BIRMINGHAM CITY
UNIVERSITY

Edgar F. Borgatta
David J. Jackson
EDITORS

AGGREGATE DATA

Analysis and Interpretation

 SAGE Publications   Beverly Hills   London

For information address:

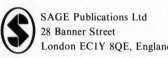

SAGE Publications, Inc.
275 South Beverly Drive
Beverly Hills, California 90212

SAGE Publications Ltd
28 Banner Street
London EC1Y 8QE, England

Printed in the United States of America

Library of Congress Cataloging in Publication Data
Main entry under title:

Aggregate data.

    Includes bibliographical references.
    1. Social sciences—Statistical methods.
I. Borgatta, Edgar F., 1924-   II. Jackson, David J.
HA29.A36   300'.1'82   79-23909
ISBN 0-8039-1428-8
ISBN 0-8039-1429-6 pbk.

FIRST PRINTING

CONTENTS

AGGREGATE DATA ANALYSIS
An Overview

EDGAR F. BORGATTA
City University of New York
DAVID J. JACKSON
National Institute of Mental Health

*i*n the social and psychological sciences, in contrast to the biological and physical sciences, being latecomers has, at times, created invidious comparisons. Because of lack of money, which may be the same as lack of credibility, the resources to do research in the social sciences have not been available, and so alternatives to direct study have been sought. Looking for other sources of available data, for those who can not collect their own, is the common alternative, and to find data in the form required is more than can be expected. Availability of aggregated data based on censuses and registrations, thus attracted many users over the history of the social sciences. The demographers are among the more prominently visible empirical researchers of the past. However, interest in topics such as suicide and anomie, mass movements, and so on relate to aggregated data available in those early days. With the wisdom of hindsight, more recent generations have been able to look back and see the methodological errors of the past in interpretation of aggregated data, and at this juncture, the questions surrounding the use of aggregated data are becoming systematized. It is to contribute to this generalization of the problem that the articles presented here have been assembled.

Some of the errors of the past have received considerable attention, and so a concept like the "ecological fallacy" is well known. Robinson's (1950) classic paper on this topic appropriately placed an important caution on the interpretation of individual-level variables based on analyses of data aggregated by geographical or other units. However, as quickly became evident, the caution became, for many, a rigid taboo on the use of aggregated data; what happened was the assumption that, because use of aggregated data could be misleading at the individual level, every such interpretation had to be incorrect. In the more tempered consideration of the problem, it became evident that: (1) while always suspect, aggregate data could suggest findings that exist at the individual level; (2) the analysis of aggregate data could be of interest in itself; (3) comparison of different levels of aggregation and individual-level data could provide interesting findings; and (4) it requires a particular brand of reductionism to attribute some characteristics associated with geographical and other aggregation units to individuals. Subsequnently, some of these topics have been considered fairly broadly, e.g., Langbein and Lichtman (1978).

The issues that are raised in dealing with aggregated data, however, proceed on to many other questions that involve assumptions about the concepts that are used, metric, and so forth. To pick a simple example, consider in an elementary way the conversion of aggregate-level data into rates. The simplest way this is done is to convert the number of cases having characteristics called Variable X_1 into a proportion, using as the denominator some basis, often the total number of observations, say Variable X_t. But, the concept that is associated with the defining of the total number of observation is often a purposeful definition, and although arbitrary in many ways, the definition may not be simple. So, for example, definition of geographical areas is not simple aggregations based on arbitrary lines, but is tied to histories that may have local aspects, may reflect time of development in the cultural history, geographical limitations, waves of migration, and so forth. The objective of some aggregate-level analysis, of course, may be designed particularly to get at this kind of suggestion by outlining the discernible principles that appear to underlie the distribution of characteristics of the geographical areas. But it is not clear, commonly, where the beginning points are and what the assumptions and purposes of the analyses are. To put it simply, if one is dealing with U.S. Census tracts, they have been defined, in part, with some original principles, such as homogeneity in mind, and with a concept of average size. During the assignment period there has been growth, and so size has varied, associated with a variety of historical circumstances, and a notion of homogeneity of size is obviously not achievable either initially or subsequently. In using size of tract as the denominator basis for rates, thus more subtle and complicated things may be occurring than simply converting another variable from a raw data form to a rate.

Aside from the complexity of process that is implied in some of the arbitrary procedures of aggregating data, sometimes the concept that is involved is not represented well by the operations involved in the creation of the measure. Thus, for example, the idea of city size may suggest many alternative measures, but for most it will conjure up an image of the metropolis as compared to a small town or city. City size is usually thought of in terms of the population size, the number of people within the geographical boundary. But, even in terms of the United States, there are immediate complexities with regard to consideration of such a variable conceptually, as there are central cities, satellites and suburb cities, fringes of various types, and so forth, and the geographical definitions in one location may have a quite different character from another. Further, if one moves out to a concept of metropolitan area or some other alternative, the rules for making boundaries become arbitrary to the point of sometimes appearing capricious. Population size is only one indication of size, and intrinsically one may be suggesting the concentration, density, with the concept rather than the total count. The concept may suggest to most people a complex of ideas, rather than a single simple measure, so that the conceptual vagueness with which much of social science appears to operate contributes directly to the kinds of errors that are made in developing measures and then reifying them.

City size thus may not be as simple a concept as it appears to be on the surface. Note that the distribution of what is called city size, when examined from the point of view of population size, is immediately a strange one. There has to be some notion of a minimum city size, and if the number is chosen relatively small, say 10,000, then the distribution by size of population begins with a pile-up at the lower end and slides down to the high end, where the largest cities would go off the chart if increments are by units of 10,000. Such a representation becomes easier by using log graph paper to attenuate the tail with only a few cities in the extreme size category. Indeed, it becomes obvious that the distribution puts only a few cases in the extremely large category, and using a metric of population size would suggest that the few large cities could often determine the correlation of that variable to another variable. The large cities operate as "outliers." But on what grounds should attenuating the distribution be considered? The answer will generally refer back to the exploration of the *concept* of city size, and, for example, one might advance a notion that city size should be seen as increasing by step increments such as small, small-medium, medium, medium large, large, and very large. This would attenuate the distribution, of course, but so would some arbitrary numerical transformation which might be applied for heuristic reasons. For example, if it is found that city size correlates with crime rate, it may be that a simple transformation on city size may eliminate the relationship, suggesting that if one takes an alternate definition of city size, the interpretation might be quite different. The question of how the allocation of numbers to the concept was done was arbitrary and intuitive to begin with, and doing other arbitrary and intuitive allocations of numbers may make as much sense, and in some cases more. Experience may be the guide in such matters, but one can only become aware of the possibilities if one is aware of the assumptions involved in the translation of the vague and intuitive concept into operations.

On the other side of the distribution, the small cities, one has to deal with the concept that at a given figure the definition starts, and below that, the units are not cities. What are they, and are a few people the difference between being a city or something else? At this point, it again becomes apparent that the intuitive notions drawn from common language lack explicitness. The whole idea of distribution of cities by size may suddenly seem like an enterprise of trying to fit literature to scientific specification. The ideal of being literary may not correspond to the demands for precision in science, and so it is possible that at some point, a different language will emerge in the science that does not correspond too well to the common language spoken.

These preliminary comments are on only one topic, but it should be seen quickly that extensions and questions for other areas will arise. The notion of groups versus individuals is shot full of problems of conceptualization, for example. The question of the "reality of groups" has been dealt with from speculative terms to dealing with issues of how characteristics of groups are to be measured independently of the characteristics of the members, sticky questions indeed.

In this context, the emphasis of the articles presented is intrinsically on the nature of measurement for aggregated data. The issues alluded to above with regard to problems associated with using rates are expanded and considered in detail, particularly with regard to the impact of the use of rates or ratios in analytical and statistical procedures that have come to the fore. Then, the issue of what is a group effect is considered, particularly in the light of "contextual analysis." The latter has had more claims for existence than evidence, and so a debate has centered not only on whether contextual effects are demonstrable, but also on whether the interpretation given to them is appropriate in the light of more general models. Additionally, assumptions of linearity in the measures used, and indeed, implicit assumptions about the nature of the relationships observed, are part and parcel of the analytic procedures that are used. The comparisons presented outline differences that may arise and how they limit applicability and interpretation.

REFERENCES

LANGBEIN, L. I. and A. J. LICHTMAN (1978) Ecological Inference. Beverly Hills, CA: Sage.
ROBINSON, W. S. (1950) "Ecological correlations and the behavior of individuals." Amer. Soc. Rev. 15: 351-356.

Edgar F. Borgatta is on the faculties of the graduate programs of Sociology and of Social Psychology and Personality at the CUNY Graduate Center. He is research director of the CASE Center for Gerontological Studies and training director of an interdisciplinary program on gerontological studies.

David J. Jackson is Associate Chief of the Population Research Section, Mental Health Study Center, National Institute of Mental Health. His research interests are factorial ecology, use of census data in mental health related research and measurement.

ASSESSING GROUP EFFECTS

2

A Comparison of Two Methods

GLENN FIREBAUGH
Vanderbilt University

Social scientists have a longstanding interest in the effects of groups independent of the personal attributes of the individuals comprising the groups (e.g., Durkheim, 1951). While this interest perhaps is greatest among sociologists (e.g., Merton and Kitt, 1950; Blau, 1960; Lazarsfeld and Menzel, 1961), discussions of group effects are not unknown in the other social sciences (e.g., Sprague, 1976; see also the selections in Dogan and Rokkan, 1974).

There are at least two reasons why the estimation of group effects is germane in social science. First, group effects are important in their own right; social context no doubt affects human behavior (Blau, 1960; Scheuch, 1974; Valkonen, 1974). Second, social scientists must sometimes rely on aggregate data in studying individuals, and the advisability of such a practice hinges on the presence of (real or spurious) group effects (Hammond, 1973; Hannan and Burstein, 1974; Firebaugh, 1978). Empirical studies of group effects, then, would be useful in gauging the likely presence and size of cross-level bias (Burstein, 1978).[1]

The purpose of this article is to explicate and compare the two regression methods most often recommended for assessing group effects in nonexperimental data: covariance analysis and contextual analysis. These methods assume that both individual-level and aggregate-level data are available;[2] the absence of individual-level data often precludes the separation of individual and group effects (Valkonen, 1974: 67-68; for a discussion of some cases where aggregate data are sufficient to estimate the independent effect of groups, see Przeworski, 1974, and its commentary in Prysby, 1976). Experts in this field should not expect to find much that is new in the ensuing discussion; I attempt only to synthesize and explicate current understanding in this area.

COVARIANCE ANALYSIS

Covariance analysis (or "analysis of covariance," often abbreviated ANCOVA) can be used to assess the effect of a nonmetric variable ("variate") on a criterion variable, controlling for metric variables ("covariates"). This technique is well-suited for multilevel analysis (i.e., analysis employing measures at different levels of aggregation), since the nonmetric variable can be an aggregate (neighborhood, precinct, church), while the metric variable can be an individual-level characteristic. The structural equation representing the effect of an aggregate-level variable, controlling for n individual-level variables, is (following Burke and Schuessler, 1974):

$$Y_{ij} = \mu + \beta_1(X_{1ij} - \bar{\bar{X}}_1) + \beta_2(X_{2ij} - \bar{\bar{X}}_2) + \ldots + \beta_n(X_{nij} - \bar{\bar{X}}_n) \quad [1]$$

$$+ \alpha_j + \epsilon_{ij}$$

$$(i = 1, 2, \ldots k; \ j = 1, 2, \ldots m)$$

where μ is common to all individuals, X_{1ij} is the score on X_1 for the ith individual in the jth group, $\bar{\bar{X}}_1$ is the grand mean of X_1, α_j is common to all individuals in the jth group, and ϵ_{ij} is specific to the ith individual in the jth group. Equation 1 states that Y is a linear and additive function of n individual-level variables ($X_1, X_2, \ldots X_n$), a group variable (α), and a random disturbance term (ϵ). We make the usual assumptions about ϵ: that it has zero mean, constant variance, is uncorrelated with the independent variables, and that the values of ϵ are mutually uncorrelated. In addition, to avoid confounding issues of multilevel analysis with those of measurement and sampling error, we assume that the variables are perfectly measured, and that equation 1 describes a population, not a sample. (To remind the reader that equation 1 is a population model, I have used Greek letters in the equation; note in particular that I am *not* using β to refer to standardized regression coefficients.)

Most pertinent to our discussion is the group variable, α. In least-squares regression analysis a constant (α_j) is fitted for each of the m groups, using the criterion that the variance of ϵ be minimized. These m constants can be estimated by using a regression equation with m-1 dummy variables (one constant is given by the y-intercept). If the constants differ, there is said to be a "group effect"[3] (for a more detailed discussion of the mechanics of covariance analysis, see Schuessler, 1971).

Three properties of the "group effect" in covariance analysis should be emphasized. First, it is a partial effect: individual-level effects are controlled (see equation 1). Second, the group effect of covariance analysis is a composite of all the relevant group-level effects. For example, suppose that mean socioeconomic status of the school, school curriculum, teacher-pupil ratio, and number of volumes in the school library all affect student's achievement test score, controlling for relevant individual-level characteristics. In such a case, the school effect obtained in covariance analysis would reflect all four group-level characteristics (assuming, of course, that the schools studied differed on all four characteristics). Third, the group effect in covariance analysis does not identify the group characteristics which affect the dependent variable. To find a school effect in a study of educational aspirations is not to identify the school characteristics (curriculum? guidance program?) which give rise to this effect. To pinpoint the relevant group characteristics, contextual analysis is more appropriate.

These points can be illustrated with two examples from sociology. In his analysis of a 1964 nationwide survey of 1,975 adults, Middleton (1976) found that antiblack prejudice was almost a standard deviation higher in the South than in the regions outside the South (Northeast, North Central, West). What accounts for this regional difference? Perhaps it is due to differences between Southerners and non-Southerners with respect to personal characteristics (education, income, and so forth) that are related to antiblack prejudice. To investigate this possibility, Middleton used covariance analysis, with controls for education, occupation, income, and size of community. This adjustment for personal characteristics failed to erase the regional difference (indeed, it narrowed the gap only slightly [Middleton, 1976: Table 4]); this finding suggests a more structural (historical-cultural) explanation for the regional difference (Middleton, 1976: 110-112).

Covariance analysis also has been used to study income differences across cities. Data collected in March, 1962, as part of the Current Population Survey indicate a disparity in income across 15 large cities for civilian male workers, aged 25-64 (N = 5,699): mean income ranged from $5,518 in Baltimore to $7,857 in Los Angeles. Does this demonstrate that there are city properties which inflate or deflate earnings independent of the backgrounds and skills of the workers, so that a given skill level is differentially rewarded across cities? Not necessarily; there may be equilibrating processes (notably migration) which "successfully . . . match city population characteristics with the city occupational structures" (Mueller, 1974: 665). In short, the observed income differences may be due entirely to differences in the personal characteristics of the workers. Mueller used covariance analysis to address this hypothesis; he found that income differences across these cities indeed were substantially reduced (but not erased entirely) by introducing controls for labor force composition.

CONTEXTUAL ANALYSIS

Boudon (1963) has suggested that, in France, the mean income of a neighborhood has a positive effect on voting behavior (conservatism), independent of individual income. A person living in a high-income neighborhood, then, is expected to vote for more conservative candidates than a person with the same income in a low-income neighborhood. In such a case, $\bar{X}$ (mean neighborhood income) would be related to Y, with X controlled. Such an effect is most often called a "contextual effect."[4]

In contextual analysis the equation analogous to equation 1 is (following Alwin, 1976: equation 15):

$$Y_{ij} = \alpha + \beta_1 X_{1ij} + \beta_2 X_{2ij} + \ldots + \beta_n X_{nij} + \beta_{n+1} \bar{X}_{1j} \qquad [2]$$

$$+ \beta_{n+2} \bar{X}_{2j} + \ldots + \beta_{2n} \bar{X}_{nj} + \epsilon_{ij}$$

$$(i = 1, 2, \ldots k; \; j = 1, 2, \ldots m)$$

where, as before, X_{1ij} represents the score on the (individual-level) variable X_1 for the ith person in the jth group. Equation 2 states that the Y score for the ith person in the jth group is a linear and additive function of n individual-level variables, n contextual variables ($\bar{X}_1$ to $\bar{X}_n$), and a random disturbance term. As in equation 1, we assume that the disturbance term has zero mean, constant variance, is uncorrelated with the independent variables, and that the values of ϵ are mutually uncorrelated. In addition, we assume (as before) that measurement error is absent and that equation 2 refers to a population. Unlike covariance analysis—where the group effect is assessed by fitting a constant for each group—in contextual analysis the group effect is assessed by n variables ($\bar{X}_1$ to $\bar{X}_n$) which are group means (Alwin, 1976).[5] $\bar{X}_{1j}$, then, represents the mean of X_1 for the jth group, and the coefficient of $\bar{X}_1$ measures the contextual effect of X_1 on Y.

We can now compare the group effect of the contextual model with that of the covariance model. In contextual analysis, as in covariance analysis, the group effect is a partial effect (see equation 2). However, contextual analysis more explicitly identifies the group characteristics involved in the group effect (Barton, 1970: 515; "The point of contextual analysis . . . [is] to find out what *general characteristics* of contexts are related to the dependent variable").

The most important difference between these two modes of analysis is that covariance analysis gives the *composite* group effect, while contextual analysis does not. We can be more specific: *the contextual effect of X is that part of the composite group effect which is associated with $\overline{X}$.* Hence, if mean religiosity of community affects church attendance over and beyond the effect of individual religiosity, such a contextual effect of religiosity can be obtained by regressing the composite community effect (represented by the fitted constants—or, equivalently, the adjusted Y-means—in covariance analysis) on the religiosity means of the communities (see Werts and Linn, 1971).

Since contextual effects are a subset of the composite group effect of covariance analysis, the variance explained by the contextual model will always be less than or equal to that explained by the corresponding covariance (or dummy variable) model (Hauser, 1971: 20). The explained variance will be equal in the very special case that the contextual variables explain all the variance in the Y-means. This is as one would expect intuitively: the contextual model, which uses continuous variables (group means) to represent the group effect, will match the fit obtained by assigning dummy variables to each group (covariance method) only when all the group means lie exactly on the regression plane. To the extent that the group means deviate from the regression plane (i.e., to the extent that $R^2_{\overline{Y} \cdot \overline{X}_1, \ldots \overline{X}_n}$ is less than unity), the contextual model loses predictive power relative to the covariance model. The chief advantage of the covariance model, then, is its greater predictive power, while the chief advantage of the contextual model is its more explicit identification of the group characteristics which affect the dependent variable.

SOME CAVEATS

Groups effects can be spurious; multilevel models can be mis-specified just like single-level models can be. Multilevel analysis, however, introduces additional issues in specification (or at least makes the issues more transparent). Discussions of specification typically focus on whether all relevant explanatory variables are included in the model, and whether these variables are incorporated in their proper mathematical form. In multilevel analysis another dimension of specification is salient: the level of aggregation of the variables. (This issue is often more acute in multilevel analyses than in single-level analyses since the proper level of aggregation is often less obvious in the former.) For example, a "school effect" could be a classroom effect in disguise; conversely, to say that there is no school effect is not to say that there is no classroom effect, or no school district effect. In short, a convincing demonstration that, for example, mean neighborhood income has an independent effect on political conservatism would require attention to the possibility that the "neighborhood income effect" (1) is not a group effect at all, but rather is an artifact of uncontrolled or inadequately controlled individual-level effects (Tannenbaum and Bachman, 1964; Hauser, 1970, 1974; Prysby, 1976); (2) is not a neighborhood *income* effect, but rather is due to the correlation between neighborhood income and other neighborhood properties which are causal (Firebaugh, 1978: Table 1); and (3) is not a *neighborhood* income effect, but rather is an income effect of some other aggregate which is correlated with neighborhood.

IMPLICATIONS AND EXTENSIONS

Decomposing composite group effects. Social scientists who study group effects encounter terms such as "contextual," "compositional," "structural," "analytical," "integral," and "aggregative" as descriptions of types of group effects which may occur. Unfortunately, the use of these terms is not consistent. While several papers have aimed to formulate consistent and complete typologies of group effects (for example, Lazarsfeld and Menzel, 1961, proposed three types of collective properties: analytical, structural, and global), no typology has gained general acceptance.

Methodologically, the important distinction is between metric and nonmetric group effects. For cities, examples of metric group characteristics include mean income, tax rate, percent black, and number of churches, while form of government, region of country, and political party in power are examples of nonmetric group characteristics (note that contextual properties are metric). The composite group effect includes the effects of both metric and nonmetric group characteristics. Hence, the independent contribution of metric and nonmetric group characteristics to the composite group effect can be assessed by regressing the adjusted Y-means on the metric and nonmetric group variables. Through this procedure of decomposing the variance explained by the nominal-scale variable (α) in equation 1, then, one can more directly assess the group properties which give rise to a (composite) group effect.

This decomposition procedure suggests that contextual analyses could be performed on published results from covariance analysis by merging the results with aggregate data. In this way the interested reader could extend the analyses even without access to the original (individual-level) data.[6] For example, one could use the adjusted income means for Mueller's (1974) cities in conjunction with ecological data on the characteristics of these cities to investigate city contextual effects on income.

Applications of the two methods. Since covariance analysis estimates the composite group effect, it is especially well-suited for predictive purposes. For example, covariance analysis would be appropriate for determining where to send one's child to school to maximize her/his expected score on some measure. (Contextual analysis, on the other hand, would be more useful in determining how to change the *school* to increase one's expected value on some measure.) Covariance analysis is also useful as a preliminary to contextual analysis. If, for example, a researcher wished to determine which school characteristics have an independent effect, covariance analysis is a useful first step. If the nominal-scale variable (school) in the covariance analysis added little explained variance, the researcher would know at the outset that none of the school characteristics could explain much additional variance in the dependent variable (see Duncan et al., 1972: ch. 7).[7]

On the other hand, if the covariance analysis showed that schools affect the dependent variable (net of individual-level variables), the researcher still would not know the causal school characteristics. Contextual analysis is useful for identifying the group characteristics which give rise to group effects. In general, then, contextual analysis is more directly applicable in causal analysis.

However, as indicated above, contextual analysis may not give a complete accounting of group effects, since the composite group effect may be caused by (metric and nonmetric) group characteristics which are not contextual. Contextual variables may be statistically significant, yet account for relatively little of the group effect. Hence covariance analysis may be useful for assessing the adequacy of the contextual model—that is, for assessing how well the contextual model fits the data relative to how well it could fit the data. In sum, the best studies of group effects incorporate both methods, since the information provided by each method is complementary.

Conclusion. Both contextual analysis and covariance analysis begin with the assumption that relevant individual-level variables are controlled and focus on the remaining group effect. However, the two methods are better suited to answer different questions. Covariance analysis asks: how large is the total impact of the groups? Contextual analysis asks: what characteristics of the groups have an effect? Often, social scientists who study group effects are interested in both questions; often, then, both methods could be usefully employed.

NOTES

1. The cross-level inference issue (e.g., Robinson, 1950) and the level of analysis issue (e.g., Singer, 1961; Eulau, 1969) are distinct from, but closely related to, the issue of estimating group effects. The level of analysis issue concerns the determination of the proper level of aggregation in research. Suppose, for example, that one is interested in decision-making in a legislative body: is the proper unit the legislator? the subcommittee? the entire legislature? The issue of cross-level inference arises if the researcher cannot collect data at the desired level of aggregation; for example, studies of individual-level correlates of voting behavior often must use data at a different level of aggregation.

2. Such data sets may be more accessible than sometimes supposed; Linz (1974), for example, gives examples of the merger of survey data and aggregate data to produce the necessary data set.

3. Note that "group effect" refers to the effect of a *variable*, not to the effect of a *particular* group.

4. Other terms which have been used include "structural effect" (Blau, 1960) and "compositional effect" (Davis et al., 1961).

5. Note that, to make this model analogous to the covariance model of equation 1, we assume that all X-variables refer to the same units. Differently stated: $\overline{X}_1$ to $\overline{X}_n$ are either all school characteristics, or all neighborhood characteristics, and so forth. In this article, then, I restrict the discussion to two-level analysis (individual and aggregate).

In addition, note that equation 2 is a "complete" contextual model (i.e., one where the n variables which have effects have *both* contextual and individual effects). Of course, "incomplete" models are also possible; in particular, one expects cases where some variables which have significant effects at the individual level have no contextual effects. Equation 2 reduces to such models by eliminating the nonsignificant terms. Hence equation 2 is the most general contextual model, and the conclusions of this article apply to contextual models in general (i.e., to incomplete as well as complete models).

6. Of course, without individual-level data the adjusted means could not be adjusted further. Hence this method is advisable only if the individual-level effects are adequately controlled—i.e., only if the reader is convinced that the group effect is not due to uncontrolled individual-level effects. I should also note that, in performing such an analysis, one should weight by group size.

7. Unfortunately, covariance analysis becomes unwieldy when the number of groups is quite large. For example, one study of school effects included over 400 schools (Hauser et al., 1976). In such a case, however, contextual analysis is not impractical.

REFERENCES

ALWIN, D. F. (1976) "Assessing school effects: some identities." Sociology of Education 49: 294-303.

BARTON, A. H. (1970) "Allen Barton comments on Hauser's 'Context and consex'." Amer. J. of Sociology 76: 514-517.

BLAU, P. M. (1960) "Structural effects." Amer. Soc. Rev. 25: 178-193.

BOUDON, R. (1963) "Proprietes individuelles et proprietes collectives: un probleme d'analyse ecologique." Revue Francaise de Sociologie 4: 275-299.

BURKE, P. J. and K. F. SCHUESSLER (1974) "Alternative approaches to analysis-of-variance tables," pp. 145-188 in H. L. Costner (ed.) Sociological Methodology 1974. San Francisco: Jossey-Bass.

BURSTEIN, L. (1978) "Alternative approaches for assessing differences between grouped and individual-level regression coefficients." Soc. Methods and Research 7: 5-28.

DAVIS, J. A., J. L. SPAETH, and C. HUSON (1961) "A technique for analyzing the effects of group composition." Amer. Soc. Rev. 26: 215-225.

DOGAN, M. and S. ROKKAN [eds.] (1974) Social Ecology. Cambridge: MIT Press.

DUNCAN, O. D., D. L. FEATHERMAN, and B. DUNCAN (1972) Socioeconomic Background and Achievement. New York: Seminar.

DURKHEIM, E. (1951) Suicide. New York: Free Press.

EULAU, H. (1969) Micro-Macro Political Analysis: Accents of Inquiry. Chicago: Aldine.

FIREBAUGH, G. (1978) "A rule for inferring individual-level relationships from aggregate data." Amer. Soc. Rev. 43: 557-572.

HAMMOND, J. L. (1973) "Two sources of error in ecological correlations." Amer. Soc. Rev. 38: 764-777.

HANNAN, M. T. and L. BURSTEIN (1974) "Estimation from grouped observations." Amer. Soc. Rev. 39: 374-392.

HAUSER, R. M. (1974) "Contextual analysis revisited." Soc. Methods and Research 2: 365-375.

——— (1971) Socioeconomic Background and Educational Performance. Washington, DC: American Sociological Association.

——— (1970) "Context and consex: a cautionary tale." Amer. J. of Sociology 75: 645-664.

——— W. H. SEWELL, and D. F. ALWIN (1976) "High school effects on achievement," in W. H. Sewell, R. M. Hauser, and D. L. Featherman (eds.) Schooling and Achievement in American Society. New York: Academic.

LAZARSFELD, P. A. and H. MENZEL (1961) "On the relation between individual and collective properties," pp. 422-440 in A. Etzioni (ed.) Complex Organizations: A Sociological Reader. New York: Holt, Rinehart & Winston.

LINZ, J. J. (1974) "Ecological analysis and survey research," in M. Dogan and S. Rokkan (eds.) Social Ecology. Cambridge: MIT Press.

MERTON, R. K. and A. S. KITT (1950) "Contributions to the theory of reference group behavior," pp. 40-105 in R. K. Merton and P. F. Lazarsfeld (eds.) Studies in the Scope and Methodology of "The American Soldier." New York: Free Press.

MIDDLETON, R. (1976) "Regional differences in prejudice." Amer. Soc. Rev. 41: 94-117.

MUELLER, C. W. (1974) "City effects on socioeconomic achievements: the case of large cities." Amer. Soc. Rev. 39: 652-667.

PRYSBY, C. L. (1976) "Community partisanship and individual voting behavior: methodological problems of contextual analysis." Pol. Methodology 3: 183-198.

PRZEWORSKI, A. (1974) "Contextual models of political behavior." Pol. Methodology 1: 27-61.

ROBINSON, W. S. (1950) "Ecological correlations and the behavior of individuals." Amer. Soc. Rev. 15: 351-357.

SCHEUCH, E. K. (1974) "Social context and individual behavior," in M. Dogan and S. Rokkan (eds.) Social Ecology. Cambridge: MIT Press.

SCHUESSLER, K. (1971) Analyzing Social Data: A Statistical Orientation. Boston: Houghton Mifflin.

SINGER, J. D. (1961) "The level of analysis problem in international relations." World Politics 14: 77-92.

SPRAGUE, J. (1976) "Estimating a Boudon-type contextual model: some practical and theoretical problems of measurement." Pol. Methodology 3: 333-353.

TANNENBAUM, A. S. and J. G. BACHMAN (1964) "Structural versus individual effects." Amer. J. of Sociology 69: 585-595.

VALKONEN, T. (1974) "Individual and structural effects in ecological research," in M. Dogan and S. Rokkan (eds.) Social Ecology. Cambridge: MIT Press.

WERTS, C. E. and R. L. LINN (1971) "Considerations when making inferences within the analysis of covariance model." Educational and Psychological Measurement 31: 407-416.

Glenn Firebaugh is an Assistant Professor of Sociology at Vanderbilt University. He is interested in Third World development, especially rural development, and is in the beginning stages of a study of the linkages between agriculture and human fertility in the Third World.

INDIVIDUALS AND SOCIAL STRUCTURE
Contextual Effects as Endogenous Feedback

3

LUTZ ERBRING
University of Michigan
ALICE A. YOUNG
Carnegie-Mellon University

*t*he impact of social structure on individual behavior has been a recurrent theme of social theory and research, from Durkheim's discussion of "social facts" onward. The sociological literature is rich in well-meaning exhortations to "bring society back in" (Barton, 1968)—especially since the advent of the sample survey. Coleman (1958) notes the pitfalls of survey research that treats individuals as though existing outside any context of social interaction. Blau (1960) points out the importance of structural

AUTHORS' NOTE: *An earlier version of this paper was presented at the 1977 Annual Meeting of the American Sociological Association, Chicago, Illinois. We are grateful to David Jackson for many helpful suggestions, and to Duane Alwin, Arthur Goldberger, and Neil Henry for comments on a previous draft.*

effects that link the distribution of personal attributes within a group to individual performance. Lazarsfeld and Menzel (1969), Davis et al. (1961), and Boudon (1967) have provided typologies of a variety of group-level effects on individual outcomes. Yet the fundamental issue of how to model the process(es) underlying social context effects has remained unresolved.

While most social scientists would probably endorse programmatic declarations about the importance of social structure, the issue becomes more difficult as soon as one presses for a specific definition of what, exactly, is meant by "social structure." Is it the *effects of social interaction* on individuals' beliefs, expectations, and behaviors as in the study of conformity, contagion, diffusion, or influence processes? Is it the particular *pattern of social relationships* that in turn constrains, channels, or otherwise determines the distribution of opportunities for such interactions? Is it the specific *content of transactions* which take place among interacting individuals that determines the effects of social structure? Must the operational concept of social structure itself be made contingent on the particular *types of social interaction* that are assumed to affect individual outcomes? Unfortunately even those who advocate the theoretical importance of social context tend to leave the meaning of their message somewhat ambiguous.

The case becomes doubly confounded in conjunction with the empirical problems of separating the effects of individual attributes from the effects of social context in the determination of individual outcomes. Here the potentially rich notion of social structure tends to become diluted into mere aggregations of individual attributes or into group-level properties in a global sense. Most assessments of "contextual effects" along these lines are represented by alternative versions of linear models in which measures of individual outcomes are regressed on combinations of individual attributes and their group-level averages. In brief, what is left of group "structure" is a simple measure of group composition: a mean score. Moreover, such studies fail to provide a consistent rationale for substantive mechanisms that might connect individual outcomes even with group composition, let alone group structure.

A number of lingering controversies have plagued this traditional formulation of "contextual effects." Thus, Hauser (1970a, 1970b, 1974) rejects the use of group averages alongside individual attributes as by-products of model underspecification at the individual level and as statistical artifacts devoid of a corresponding substantive process. Alwin (1976) has further clarified the algebraic relationships between several alternative specifications of this type which have commonly been employed to estimate contextual effects. Campbell and Alexander (1965) and Alexander and McDill (1976) argue that the effects of group structure on individual outcomes are mediated through interaction with "significant others" and thus should be represented by the mean values of the attributes of relevant peers rather than of the entire group. Finally, Hannan et al. (1976) demonstrate the importance of the choice of level of analysis and of the inclusion of all relevant independent variables in the analysis.

In this article we focus on the nature of intervening mechanisms that mediate the effect of social structure on individual outcomes. We attempt to show that this focus is helpful in making the necessary transition from estimating contextual effects to providing contextual explanations. We shall illustrate our argument with alternative explanations that have been discussed in the study of school effects, though our conclusions are applicable to a large variety of substantive problems involving contextual effects.

A careful examination of alternative mechanisms through which school context effects on individual aspirations or achievements might come about reveals that the specifications usually employed to model these effects are inaccurate representations of the manner in which group structure may affect individual outcomes. We then propose a class of endogenous feedback models that do provide an adequate formalization of contextual effects and permit, indeed require, the inclusion of social structure as an explicit part of model specification. We also discuss some special estimation problems raised by this new model and present several approaches for dealing with them.

AN ANALYSIS OF CONTEXTUAL MECHANISMS

If social context is to affect individual behavior, such effects must be mediated through processes that are somehow contingent upon the social structure in which the individual is embedded. Thus, a specification of group-level effects on individual outcomes requires, first of all, a careful examination of possible linkage mechanisms through which the hypothesized "contextual effects" might operate. In particular, we shall argue that contextual effects must be conceptualized as a consequence of processes of interaction among individuals in a social network. Interaction may involve either actual face-to-face contact between pairs of individuals or symbolic categorical relations shared among all individuals in a given group. Face-to-face interaction would give rise to social processes of contagion (diffusion, persuasion) underlying such group phenomena as assimilation (conformity, consensus, "pull") and contrast (polarization, differentiation, "push"). Symbolic interaction would give rise to social-psychological processes of comparison underlying such "reference group" phenomena as competition, emulation, identification, facilitation and inhibition. Without reference to social interaction in either form, the notion of contextual effects tends to become theoretically vacuous.

The traditional treatment of contextual effects has proceeded from a statistical formalization based on "individual-effect-plus-group-effect" to the imputation of alternative contextual mechanisms purporting to explain or account for statistical results. In this section we shall pursue a different strategy by examining the relationship between formal specifications and substantive mechanisms from two perspectives: (1) treating the conventional statistical model of contextual effects as a structural specification, what substantive mechanisms are implied? (2) treating alternative conventional interpretations of contextual effects as substantive mechanisms, what structural specifications are implied, and how are they related to the traditional formulation?

CONVENTIONAL FORMULATION: SOCIAL TELEPATHY

Stripped to its bare bones, the standard contextual effects model can be represented by the following structural equation:

$$y_{ij} = a + b_1 x_{ij} + b_2 \bar{x}_{.j} + e_{ij} \qquad [1]$$

where y_{ij} might represent the academic achievement of the ith student in the jth class, x_{ij} might be a measure of intellectual ability for the same student, and $\bar{x}_{.j}$ would be the average value of student ability in the jth class; e_{ij} is an error term representing all unspecified causes of y_{ij}. The coefficients a, b_1, and b_2 can be estimated by ordinary least squares regression if the usual OLS assumptions about the error terms can be justified (i.e., the e_{ij} have zero expected value, are independent and homoskedastic across all values of i and j, and are independent of x_{ij} and of $\bar{x}_{.j}$).

In order to highlight the implications of the model specified in equation 1, let us first write the average ability score, $\bar{x}_{.j}$, explicitly as the mean of individual student scores, i.e.,

$$y_{ij} = a + b_1 x_{ij} + (b_2/n_j)[x_{1j} + \ldots + x_{ij} + \ldots + x_{n_j j}] + e_{ij} \qquad [2]$$

where n_j is the number of students in the jth class. By collecting terms for the ith student and for all other (i'^{th}) students in the jth class, equation 2 becomes

$$y_{ij} = a + (b_1 + b_2/n_j)x_{ij} + (b_2/n_j) \sum_{i' \neq i} x_{i'j} + e_{ij} \qquad [3]$$

or

$$y_{ij} = a + b_1^* x_{ij} + b_2 \bar{x}_{i'j} + e_{ij} \qquad [4]$$

where

$$b_1^* = (b_1 + b_2/n_j) \quad \text{and} \quad \bar{x}_{i'j} = (1/n_j) \sum_{i' \neq i} x_{i'j}.$$

While the performance of a given student (i) is affected by *all* other students $(i' \neq i)$ in the jth class, we shall confine our graphical representations to a single peer (i′) only, for the sake of simplicity; thus, for any given student (i), the model implied by equation 1 can be diagrammed as shown in Figure 1. Equation 1 evidently implies the *direct* flow of effects from (each) student (i′)'s ability to student (i)'s performance, and similarly from student (i)'s ability to (each) student (i′)'s performance *without,* in either case, letting this impact on performance be mediated by the student's own ability.

Now, it is possible to conceive of perverse situations in which one student's ability directly causes another student's performance. Honor Code scandals at West Point (or the existence of disciplinary sanctions against cheating in less prominent citadels of learning) exemplify that possibility. Once universal cheating is ruled out, however, the proponents of such a model of contextual effects must, in fact, rely on social telepathy as an intervening mechanism. Yet "action at a distance" is a well-known principle of magic, not of science which, on the contrary, is premised on the denial of that possibility and the search for intervening links.

The elevation of social telepathy to the status of an explanatory principle is by no means specific to the particular example above. Thus, let y_{ij} be student aspirations rather than performance and x_{ij} parental SES, with $\bar{x}_{.j}$ as the school mean of parents' SES. To justify the direct effects model of equation 1, we must again either make rather implausible assumptions about the incidence and impact of contact between each student and all *other* students' parents, or invoke action at a distance. Or finally, let y_{ij} be student performance as before, and x_{ij} student aspirations, with $\bar{x}_{.j}$ the mean aspiration levels by class. Once again, we are left with the need to postulate implausible linkage mechanisms such as vicarious gratification in order to rationalize the impact of other students' aspirations on each student's performance, or we must insist on social telepathy as an explanatory principle.

Incidentally, the problem does not go away by stipulating that it is not the characteristics of *all* other students in the group (class or school, as the case may be) but only of those "relevant peers" which exert direct influence on one's own performance (see, e.g., Campbell and Alexander, 1965; Alexander and McDill, 1976). It

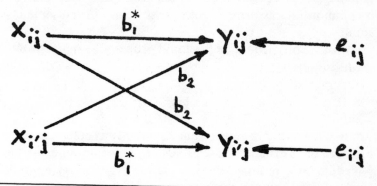

Figure 1: Social Telepathy Model of Direct Effects

is undoubtedly true that the indiscriminate inclusion of every other student's score in each student's equation (as in the case of class or school averages) is particularly unrealistic in many cases. Yet the restriction to "relevant peers" (those students with whom the individual interacts) does not eliminate the direct effects assumption of equation 1 and hence the problem of postulating implausible generating mechanisms to account for peer effects.

CONVENTIONAL INTERPRETATIONS

In considering alternative models, we direct our attention to the more plausible types of contextual mechanisms which have in fact been proposed, often in conjuction with the use of equation 1 in practice. We shall refer to them as "common fate" and "group norms," respectively, and present the corresponding structural specifications, in order to discuss their formal and statistical properties in light of the formalization of equation 1.

Common fate. Let us first consider the possibility of intervening mechanisms through which each student's performance might be at least *indirectly* affected by every other student's ability, as stipulated by the inclusion of group mean ability in equation 1. Thus, the average ability of students in a class might have a positive effect on the quality of instruction, e.g., by increasing pace of coverage, teacher enthusiasm, and so on. These global effects are presumably experienced by all students alike, as a common fate associated with membership in the same classroom.

Consequently, equation 1 should properly be replaced by the specification:

$$y_{ij} = a + b_1 x_{ij} + c z_j + e'_{ij} \qquad [5]$$

where y_{ij} and x_{ij} are achievement and ability as before, and z_j is a measure of instructional treatment; e'_{ij} is again an error term. Note that no $\bar{x}_j$ term appears in equation 5. For any given student (i) and (each) peer (i'), the model associated with equation 5 can be diagrammed as shown in Figure 2. Of course, the common fate variable may also be defined at the school level rather than the classroom level; thus, if y_{ij} is academic performance but x_{ij} is parent SES, then z_j might represent the impact of institutional resource endowments (assuming that dollars do make a difference as school administrators insist).

Clearly, if instruction quality or school resources are the postulated intervening mechanisms, direct measures of those variables should be used for z_j. Thus, quality of instruction could be represented in the model by measures such as amount of teacher time devoted to class preparation, amount of curricular material covered, or the like; similarly, resource endowments could be represented by a measure such as budget expenditures per student.

The implication of this type of intervening mechanism is, of course, that class average ability or school mean SES terms in equation 1 act merely as proxies for an intervening global variable such as instructional quality or school resources. Under these circumstances, any apparent "group effect" in the form of $b_2\bar{x}_{i'j}$ in equation 4 would be indirect at best and would in fact conceal the nature of the intervening common-fate variable directly responsible for the outcome.[1] Moreover, the common fate model is not necessarily consistent even with an interpretation in terms of indirect effects of $x_{i'j}$ on y_{ij} mediated by z_j. For example, let y_{ij} be achievement and x_{ij} aspirations, but assume that z_j represents

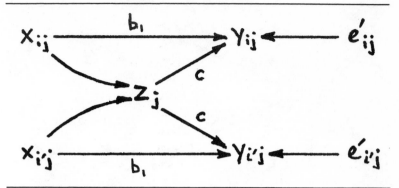

Figure 2: Common Fate Model of Indirect Effects

"exogenous" teacher characteristics (e.g., personal charisma). In that case, the common-fate variable would be a cause—rather than a consequence—of individual aspirations (as shown in Figure 3). To be sure, average aspiration level might still act as a proxy for teacher characteristics, but now the apparent effects of $x_{i'j}$ on y_{ij} would be spurious rather than indirect (due to their joint dependence on z_j).

Evidently, the common fate model does not represent a contextual process that involves the presence of others in any essential way. Rather, it remains strictly a case of individual effects, in a situation in which many individuals happen to share identical scores on a "contextual" variable, z, whose effects occur entirely at the individual level.

Group norms. A rather different intervening mechanism comes into view if we consider the possible role of "group norms" which are often credited as a source of contextual effects. Thus, suppose y_{ij} represents achievement and x_{ij} represents aspirations as before, such that the scores of all students taken together might be interpreted as defining group "norms" or "climate" with respect to educational values. Evidently, if this "climate" is to have an effect on individual performance, such an effect must be understood as the result of processes of social interaction among students. By rejecting the possibility of a *direct* impact of one stu-

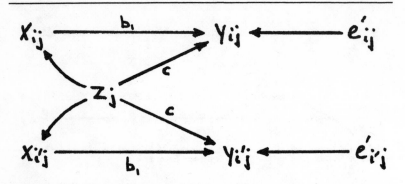

Figure 3: Common Fate Model of Spurious Effects

dent's aspirations on another's achievements as "social telepathy" we have not, of course, ruled out the possibility that such an effect could occur *indirectly,* via the impact of peer aspirations on one's own *aspirations.* Indeed the manner in which attitude and value consensus may emerge from the process of interaction among individuals suggests that the underlying model is one of mutual influence among peers, as diagrammed in Figure 4.

If the model in Figure 4 correctly represents the operation of value climates in the process of student achievement, then the corresponding specification is given by:

$$y_{ij} = a + b_1 x_{ij} + e_{ij}'' \qquad [6]$$

Note that there is no direct effect of $x_{i'j}$ on y_{ij}; rather, the effect of $x_{i'j}$ on y_{ij} is mediated entirely through that of the individual determinant x_{ij}. Consequently, no group average term $\bar{x}_{.j}$ appears in equation 6. In other words, one student's aspirations are assumed to influence another student's achievements only insofar as they modify the latter's aspirations. In turn the latter's aspirations generally affect performance, at the individual level, no matter what combination of background factors (including peer aspirations) may have helped to shape them.

To be sure, equation 1 misrepresents the process of Figure 4, which in reality implies a zero coefficient for the group mean

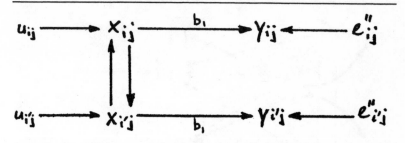

Figure 4: Social Norms Model of Indirect Effects

variable (the term $\bar{x}_{i'j}$ in equation 4). In practice, the implications of the structural model may easily be clouded by errors of measurement if a researcher has used imperfect indicators of the exogenous variable, x_{ij}. Suppose y_{ij} is achievement, while x_{ij}^* represents the set of educational values and aspirations typically associated with family background and measured by an imperfect indicator, x_{ij}, such as parental SES. Now, while interaction among students may affect student values—the "true" exogenous variable—that process will obviously not alter their parents' SES, as shown in Figure 5. Therefore, the effects of interaction on the true scores, x_{ij}^*, will not be reflected by the measured scores, x_{ij}.

If student values, x_{ij}^*, had been measured directly, their effect on achievement would be estimated correctly by the coefficient $b_1^\dagger$ in Figure 5, and the effects of exogenous feedback involving the x_{ij}^* would remain outside the model, as in equation 6. The consequences of using the indicator x_{ij} instead are twofold. First, the impact of student values is underestimated by the coefficient b_1; second, and more importantly, the impact of other student values $x_{i'j}^*$ (actually zero) will be overestimated. The result will be the misleading appearance of a separate effect based on the group average $\bar{x}_{i'j}$ of the indicator variable, as in equation 4, since the indirect effect of other student values $x_{i'j}^*$ on performance is not mediated by the measured scores, x_{ij}.[2] Of course, the preferred strategy again is the use of a direct measure of the relevant construct, e.g., individual student values, not parent SES; alternatively, an unbiased estimate of b_1 could be obtained (e.g., via

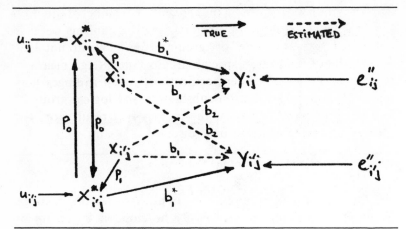

Figure 5: Social Norms Model with Measurement Error

LISREL) by using *both* x_{ij} and $\bar{x}_{i'j}$ as fallible indicators of the unobserved variable x^*_{ij}.

Unlike the intervening mechanisms considered previously, the present case—feedback among the "exogenous" variables—involves a genuine contextual process: interaction among individuals within a particular social structure. However, the effects of that process remain entirely hidden from view: the impact of social context on individual outcomes is confined to variables which are "exogenous" with respect to the outcome variable of interest, i.e., the impact of $x_{i'j}$ on x_{ij} cannot be represented in a model in which y_{ij} is the dependent variable.

SUMMARY

The result of our examination of alternative contextual mechanisms thus far may be stated succinctly. On the one hand, we have shown that as a structural model the traditional formulation of "individual effect plus group effect" models implies rather implausible generating mechanisms for contextual effects ("social telepathy"). On the other hand, we have found that interpretrations which lead to more plausible alternative generating mechanisms are incompatible with the traditional specification, since the group mean terms in the conventional model of equation 1 cannot be derived from the intervening mechanisms we have considered ("common fate" or "group norms"). We do not deny the possibility that under special circumstances (e.g., measurement error or model underspecification) group averages may appear in estimation. But on substantive and logical grounds, they have no place in any of the models that result from the intervening mechanisms we have discussed thus far.

ENDOGENOUS FEEDBACK

SOCIAL CONTAGION PROCESSES

We have argued earlier that the notion of contextual effects requires explicit assumptions about, and models of, social interaction among individuals. Therefore, we now introduce an alternative intervening mechanism through which contextual effects could arise as a result of social interaction among individuals. This type of mechanism underlies such social processes as contagion, facilitation, competition, or conformity, all of which lend specific meaning to the notion of "contextual effects." What characterizes these and many other social phenomena is the idea of reciprocal influence or mutual adjustment of individuals interacting with each other. Individual behavior is assumed to be both passively responsive to the contextual cues provided by the behavior of significant others, and at the same time actively impinging upon the behavior of others sharing the same social environment.

We shall refer to the class of situations involving such processes of contextual interaction as cases of endogenous feedback, since the behavioral outcomes of interest represented by the endogenous variable are assumed to be interdependent, in addition to incorporating the effects of one or more exogenous variables. Thus suppose y_{ij} is achievement and x_{ij} is ability. This time, however, we assume that the performance of one student is affected by the *performance* (rather than a background characteristic) of another, and vice versa. The resulting model can be diagrammed as in Figure 6. Note that the same model would be appropriate without regard to the particular exogenous variables involved; thus in a model for student achievement, x_{ij} might represent student ability, student aspirations, parent SES, or whatever. Note also that the substantive process involved (social contagion) is the same as that assumed above ("social norms"), and the model would indeed have been appropriate there if student values had been the *dependent* variable in the earlier case.

The formal specification corresponding to this model is characterized by two essential features. First, it includes terms in $y_{i'j}$ in the equation for y_{ij}, where (i′) represents the relevant peers with whom (i) interacts; this has important implications for the error terms, u_{ij}, which are discussed more fully below. Second, the model incorporates explicit assumptions for each (i) about who the relevant peers (i′) are; thus the "social structure" through which the particular effects are mediated becomes an integral part of the specification of the model, as suggested by the $w_{ii'}$ terms (and their associated coefficient, α). Since this endogenous feedback model is new to the contextual effects literature, we provide a more complete presentation of its specification and estimation below.

SPECIFICATION OF THE MODEL

We begin by considering the specification of the endogenous feedback model in Figure 6. Let us assume that the data consist of observations for all students in m classrooms, with n_j students per class. Our contextual hypothesis states that the achievement of the ith student in the jth classroom, y_{ij}, is a function of his or her own academic ability, x_{ij} *and* of the *achievement,* $y_{i'j}$, of those other students (i′) with whom the ith student interacts, with connectivity $w_{(ij)(i'j')}$. These assumptions imply the following specification of the model:[3]

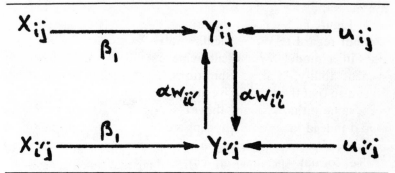

Figure 6: Endogenous Feedback Model of Social Conformity

$$y_{ij} = \alpha \left(\sum_{j'=1}^{m} \sum_{i'=1}^{n_{j'}} w_{(ij)(i'j')} \, y_{i'j'} \right) + \beta_0 + \beta_1 x_{ij} + u_{ij}, \qquad [7]$$

$$(i = 1, \ldots, n_j; \quad j = 1, \ldots, m)$$

Here, a and β_1 are the regression coefficients corresponding to the terms

$$\left(\sum_{j'=1}^{m} \sum_{i'=1}^{n_{j'}} w_{(ij)(i'j')} \, y_{i'j'} \right)$$

and x_{ij}, respectively; α is a feedback coefficient representing the effect of mutual interaction among students, and β_1 is an impact coefficient representing the effect of a student's individual ability. $w_{(ij)(i'j')}$ is a weight pertaining to the extent of interaction between student i of class j and student i' of class j'; for two students who do not interact, $w_{(ij)(i'j')} = 0$, and $w_{(ij)(ij)} = 0$ by definition. u_{ij} is an independently distributed error term.

The general form of the model in equation 7 (assuming for convenience from here on that $n_1 = n_2 = \ldots = n_j = n$, with $mn = N$) is given by

$$y = \alpha W y + X \beta + u, \qquad [8]$$

where:

> y is an N by 1 vector of outcome scores, y_{ij},
>
> X is an N by P matrix of exogenous variables, which could include a constant term;
>
> α is the feedback coefficient;
>
> β is a P by 1 vector of regression coefficients for the exogenous variables;
>
> W is an N by N matrix of fixed weights representing the structure of interaction through which the N units of observation are connected with each other, with zeros along the main diagonal;
>
> u is an N by 1 vector of disturbances, u_{ij}, with $u \sim N(0, \sigma^2 I)$. (I is the identity matrix.)

The structure of the *contiguity matrix, W,* is an integral part of the model. In general, W represents exogenous information about physical or social contiguity among members of the collectivity. Thus, it mirrors an essential aspect of the social structure characterizing a particular population and it defines the conduit for a variety of substantive processes which involve interaction among individuals—persuasion, contagion, competition, cooperation, emulation, and so on. Clearly, W has to be specified a priori, either on the basis of data about the incidence of relevant pairwise contacts among students or, in the absence of more specific information, by resorting to simplifying assumptions about patterns of social interaction.

The definition of contiguity may vary depending on the type of process assumed to generate the contextual feedback effects. Thus, in the case of communication or contagion processes, contiguity may be based explicitly on amount of face-to-face interaction specific to each pair of students; whereas in the case of comparison or competition processes, contiguity may be defined as fixed and equal for all pairs of students in a given classroom and zero for all pairs of students from different classrooms. Moreover, the latter case of equal within-class contiguity and zero between-class contiguity may also be a plausible assumption about the probability of face-to-face interaction in the absence of further information.

In conjunction with the appropriate contiguity matrix W, the *feedback rate* α is of critical importance from a substantive point of view. It provides a measure of the extent to which the outcome variable for each individual, e.g., academic performance, is affected by contiguous "spillover" from other members of the group.[4] Specifically, if the rows of W are normalized to sum to unity, e.g., by expressing each individual's amount of contact with others in terms of proportions, then the metric of the dependent variable is preserved by the endogenous feedback term. As a result, α can be interpreted as the share of individual outcomes y_{ij} determined by contextual as opposed to individual mechanisms.

In its general form, the endogenous feedback model defines an entire class of processes characterized by "social contagion" phenomena. Formally, $y_i = \alpha y_i'$ states that for $\alpha > 0$ the impact of y_i' on y_i will be directly proportional to the score of y_i', while for $\alpha < 0$ the impact of y_i' will be inversely proportional to y_i'. Substantively the model specializes to distinct processes by virtue of alternative definitions of the sensitivity parameter α. Thus, consensus processes (assimilation) take the form $y_i = \lambda(y_i' - y_i)$ while polarization processes (contrast) take the form $y_i = \lambda(y_i - y_i')$, with $0 < \lambda < 1$ in both cases. In the former case, the effect of y_i' on y_i is positive for $y_i < y_i'$ and negative for $y_i > y_i'$ (y_i moves *closer* to y_i'); in the latter case, the opposite holds: the effect of y_i' on y_i is positive if $y_i' < y_i$ and negative if $y_i > y_i'$ (y_i moves *away* from y_i'). Simple algebraic manipulation then leads to the following results for

(a) assimilation:

$$y_i = \lambda(y_i' - y_i)$$

$$(1 + \lambda)y_i = \lambda y_i'$$

$$y_i = \lambda/(\lambda + 1)y_i'$$

(b) contrast:

$$y_i = \lambda(y_i - y_i')$$

$$(1 - \lambda)y_i = -\lambda y_i'$$

$$y_i = \lambda/(\lambda - 1)y_i'$$

Thus, both cases are readily subsumed under the general form of the contagion model such that $\alpha = \lambda/(\lambda + 1) > 0$ represents "consensus" processes and $\alpha = \lambda/(\lambda - 1) < 0$ represents "polarization" processes.

In order to appreciate the role of the endogenous feedback component of the model in the contextual determination of individual outcomes, it is instructive to rearrange the terms in equation 8 to give:

$$(I - \alpha W)y = X\beta + u \qquad [9]$$

Equation 9 expresses the dependent variable, net of feedback effects, as a function of the exogenous variables and the disturbances. Now, the reduced form of equation 9 is

$$y = (I - \alpha W)^{-1}\beta + (I - \alpha W)^{-1}u \qquad [10]$$

Note that the inverse matrix in equation 10 is the limit of a convergent infinite series of the form

$$(I - \alpha W)^{-1} = I + \alpha W + (\alpha W)^2 + \ldots$$

provided that $-1 < \alpha < 1$. Thus, equation 10 can be written as

$$y = X\beta + (\alpha W)X\beta + (\alpha W)^2 X\beta + \ldots + (I - \alpha W)^{-1}u \qquad [11]$$

Formally, equation 11 represents the equilibrium of the feedback structure of the model.[5] Substantively, equation 11 illustrates that the final scores on the endogenous variables incorporate the results of cumulative "filtering" of the effects of exogenous variables, including their direct impact on each individual member of the group; their indirect effects due to the impact of exogenous variables on those with whom s/he interacts, on those with whom his/her first-order interaction partners interact, and so on.

ESTIMATION OF THE MODEL

Ordinary least squares estimation of α and β from equation 8 would produce inconsistent estimates of model parameters. Since a linear combination of observations for the dependent variable appears on the right hand side of equation 8, there is feedback between the regressors and the error term in the model. This violation of the standard OLS assumptions becomes evident upon closer examination of Figure 6. The figure shows the feedback process involving the respective academic achievement levels of students in a class j which consists of two individuals, i and i', who interact with one another with relative frequencies, $w_{ii'}$ and $w_{i'i}$ (and who have no significant contact outside their class). It can be seen that the impact of the performance of (i') on that of (i) is confounded with the disturbance u_{ij}, which becomes part of $y_{i'j}$ by virtue of the latter's dependence on y_{ij}; the same holds true for the impact of the performance of (i) on that of (i'), with respect to the disturbance $u_{i'j}$. Thus, the model is a simultaneous equation structure, and the endogenous variable must be purged of feedback effects before consistent estimates of α and of β can be obtained.

In order to address the estimation problem, it is useful to proceed from the rearranged form of the basic model given by equation 9 above, which expresses the dependent variable, net of feedback effects, as a function of the exogenous variables and disturbances. If an estimate of α could be secured separately and if the existence of the inverse matrix $(I - \alpha W)^{-1}$ was assured, then the remaining parameters could be estimated (conditional on a fixed value of α) from the reduced form in equation 10, by applying the appropriate transformation to the exogenous variables. But the resulting estimates would still not be consistent, since the reduced-form transformation would necessarily destroy the independence property for the transformed disturbances, i.e.,

$$E\left[(I-\alpha W)^{-1}uu'(I-\alpha W)^{-1'}\right] = (I-\alpha W)^{-1} E\left[uu'\right](I-\alpha W)^{-1'}$$

$$= (\sigma^2 I)\left[(I-\alpha W)'(I-\alpha W)\right]^{-1}$$

which is a nondiagonal matrix.

A maximum likelihood estimation procedure that avoids the disturbance problems associated with reduced-form estimation in this case has been proposed recently by Ord (1975). The ML estimator can be derived directly from the rearranged form of the structural model in equation 9 above, i.e.,

$$Ay = X\beta + u$$

where $A = (I - \alpha W)$.

Since this specification contains the structural disturbances, the original assumption of independently and identically distributed errors is preserved. It follows that the likelihood of $y^\circ = Ay$ is a function of the density of u, where $u = Ay - X\beta$. Assuming $f(u) \sim N[0, \sigma^2 I]$, therefore,

$$L[y^\circ] = L(Ay) = (2\pi\sigma^2)^{-N/2} \exp[-(1/2\sigma^2)(Ay - X\beta)'(Ay - X\beta)]. \quad [12]$$

The dependent variable y° is unobserved since it contains the unknown parameter α, but the observed y, which do not contain the unknown parameter α, are linear transforms of the y . Thus, using the Jacobian of the transformation $y^\circ = Ay$, the resulting likelihood function of y is

$$L[y] = L[y^\circ]\left|\left(\mathrm{Det}\,\frac{\partial y^\circ}{\partial y}\right)\right| = L[Ay]\,|\mathrm{Det}(A)| \qquad [13]$$

$$= (2\pi\sigma^2)^{-N/2}\exp[-(1/2\sigma^2)(Ay - X\beta)'(Ay - X\beta)]\,|\mathrm{Det}(A)|$$

yielding the log-likelihood function

$$L^*[\alpha,\beta,\sigma^2;y] = (-N/2)\ln(2\pi\sigma^2) - (1/2\sigma^2)[(Ay - X\beta)'(Ay - X\beta)] \quad [14]$$

$$+ \ln|\mathrm{Det}(A)|.$$

Maximizing L* with respect to β and σ^2 yields the maximum likelihood estimators

$$\hat{\beta} = (X'X)^{-1}X'Ay \qquad [15]$$

and, using equation 15,

$$\hat{\sigma}^2 = [y'A'MAy]/N \qquad [16]$$

where

$$M = (I - X(X'X)^{-1}X').$$

These estimators are conditional upon α, which must be estimated by iterative grid search based on its concentrated likelihood function. The concentrated log-likelihood function for α, using equations 15 and 16, is given by

$$L^*[\alpha; y, \hat{\beta}, \hat{\sigma}^2] = [N/2(1 + \ln(2\pi))] - (N/2) \ln[\sigma^2 |\operatorname{Det}(A)|^{-2/N}] \qquad [17]$$

Thus the solution is equivalent to finding the smallest value of $y'A'MAy / |\operatorname{Det}(A)|^{2/N}$.

The procedure suggested by Ord (1975) is based on the eigenvalues of W. It avoids the need to evaluate the determinant of $A = (I - \alpha W)$ afresh for each trial value of α, and thus makes maximum likelihood estimation computationally feasible. Briefly, the eigenvalues λ_i of W are the roots of the polynomial

$$|\lambda I - W| = 0 \qquad [18]$$

which can be factored into

$$\Pi_i(\lambda - \lambda_i) = 0 \qquad [19]$$

whence

$$|\lambda I - W| = \prod_i(\lambda - \lambda_i). \qquad [20]$$

Since the eigenvalues λ^* of αW are proportional by α to those of W, such that

$$| \lambda^*I - \alpha W| = \prod_i(\lambda^* - \alpha\lambda_i) \qquad [21]$$

it follows that the required determinant is given by

$$| I - \alpha\ W| = \prod_i(1 - \alpha\lambda_i). \qquad [22]$$

Consequently, the quantity which is to be maximized by $\hat{\alpha}$ in equation 17 is given by

$$Min[Q/R]$$

where

$$R = [\prod_i (1 - \alpha\lambda_i)]^{2/N},$$

while

$$Q = y'A'MAy = y'My - 2\alpha y'MWy + \alpha^2 y'W'Wy.$$

Note that Q is simply the error sum of squares resulting from $\hat{\beta}$ in equation 15. The evaluation of the λ_i, in turn, may be further simplified, especially for large matrices, if W can be forced into block-diagonal form such that eigenvalues can be obtained separately for each block. Even where this is not possible, computation may be simplified if W contains a large number of zero cells as will often be the case in practice.

In sum, endogenous feedback models not only provide a theoretical specification of contextual effects; they are now also well within reach of practical estimation.

SPECIFICATION BIAS

Before concluding our discussion of estimation issues, it may be useful to consider the implications of a particular case of specification error which appear to be at the heart of the statistical debate over "contextual effects" associated with the traditional formulation of equation 1. This is the case where the correct model is really the endogenous feedback model,

$$y = \alpha Wy + X\beta + u \qquad [u \sim \text{IID}] \qquad [23]$$

but estimation is based instead on the underspecified "model"

$$y = X\beta + v \qquad [24]$$

which implies that

$$v = \alpha Wy + u. \qquad [25]$$

Now, substituting for y in equation 25 reveals that the error process has the form

$$v = \alpha W(X\beta + v) + u \qquad [26]$$

with the result that estimates of β from equation 24 will be biased and inconsistent since X enters into, and hence is necessarily correlated with, v. Moreover, equation 24 can be written as

$$y = X\beta + [\alpha WX\beta + \alpha Wv + u] \qquad [27]$$

with the consequence that, *if* (for whatever reason) a term in WX were added to the underspecified "model" of equation 24, then the resulting estimating equation

$$y = X\beta + \alpha WX\beta + v^* \qquad [v^* = \alpha Wv + u] \qquad [28]$$

would lead to a substantively meaningless (spurious) coefficient estimate associated with WX (which in any case would be a biased and inconsistent estimate of $\alpha\beta$ since, from equation 26, WX is correlated with the disturbance term v^* in equation 28). Further discussion of autocorrelated error structures in contextual models is provided in the Appendix.[6]

The relationship between the conventional "group mean" formulations of "contextual effects" and the omission of underlying endogenous feedback from the model can be brought into sharper focus by considering the bias effect of that specification error in the context of OLS estimation. Obviously the effects of the specification bias in equation 24 depend on the form of W (recall that there are a number of different ways to specify W). For purposes of exposition we only consider the special case in which pairs of student interactions are equally weighted within classrooms, while no significant interaction occurs across classrooms. This specification is most readily tractable and corresponds to the typical design for conventional discussions of contextual effects at the "group" level.

Thus, we assume that, for a given school, W is a block-diagonal matrix containing blocks of $(\ell\ell'/n)$ on the diagonal (where ℓ is a vector of unities).[7] For this definition of W, the basic model of equation 23 becomes

$$y = \alpha\bar{y} + X\beta + u \qquad [29]$$

where

$$\bar{y} = I \otimes (\ell\ell'/n)y = Wy$$

is a vector of group means and $\otimes$ denotes the Kronecker product. Accordingly, the expectation of the OLS estimator for the incorrectly specified model in equation 24

$$E(\hat{\beta}) = \beta + E[(X'X)^{-1}X'\alpha Wy] \qquad [30]$$

reduces to

$$E(\hat{\beta}) = \beta + E[(X'X)^{-1}X'\bar{y}]\alpha. \qquad [31]$$

Now, if the model without the endogenous feedback term were to be estimated from a "partitioned" (within-group) design, separately for each of the j classrooms, then the bias in equation

31 would remain confined to an intercept shift (since $\bar{y}_{\cdot j}$ is constant within a given group).[8] In fact even if the theoretically appropriate feedback term $\alpha\bar{y}$ were included, the vector of $\bar{y}_{\cdot j}$ would be indistinguishable from the constant term of the model in each group, and an estimate of α could not be obtained (i.e., the data matrix would be singular). Thus, while the omission of endogenous feedback from the specification will result in group-specific intercept biases, estimates of exogenous impact coefficients would remain unbiased under a "within" design.

If instead the model without the endogenous feedback term were to be estimated from a "total" (all groups combined) design, the bias in equation 31 would extend to the coefficient estimates for the exogenous variables. The reason for the latter effect becomes readily apparent by recognizing, first, that the term $(X'X)^{-1}X'\bar{y}$, which controls the bias in equation 31 above, is simply the regression of group means $\bar{y}_{\cdot j}$ on the exogenous variables; and second, that this regression is necessarily nonzero whenever the regression of individual scores, y_{ij}, on the same exogenous variables (i.e., $(X'X)^{-1}X'\bar{y}$ in general) is nonzero to begin with.[9] Thus under a "total" analysis design the omission of endogenous feedback from the specification will lead to biased estimates of the impact of exogenous variables on individual outcomes.

There are several estimation strategies which might serve to purge coefficients for the exogenous variables of the bias resulting from omission of the endogenous feedback component. One of these would be to use a pooled design with a more complex error structure which acknowledges the existence of unspecified group-level effects, e.g., in the form of group-specific dummy variables. While this removes the bias from the coefficient estimates for the exogenous variables, it does not eliminate bias from the model altogether; it merely reallocates it to the "group" intercept terms (thus paralleling the results obtained from partitioned estimation). Furthermore, this approach precludes any possibility of distinguishing this particular source of bias from the effects of other possible specification errors, all of which are confounded by fitting group-specific intercepts.

A second strategy which might help compensate for the omission of endogenous feedback would be to introduce the group means of the *exogenous* variable(s) as additional regressor(s) in the total design, as in equation 1. Recalling that the omitted feedback term, i.e., the group mean of the endogenous variable, is necessarily correlated with the group means of the exogenous variable(s) in the model, the latter in effect become proxies of the former during estimation. This estimation procedure extracts the bias from the estimated structural coefficients and converts it into coefficient estimates associated with the group means (which yield, in effect, partial intercept shifts for the groups).[10] The result is essentially equivalent to the addition of group dummy variables except that it avoids the "over-fitting" of the former approach. Unlike the use of dummy variables, however, it invites substantive interpretations in terms of "group-level effects" of exogenous variables which, under the circumstances, are evidently spurious. Yet it is just this statistical relationship which appears to underlie the traditional formulation of "contextual effects" as in equation 1.

The third strategy, and obviously the one which we would advocate, is to eliminate the bias at the outset by proper specification of the model, i.e., by allowing for the possibility of endogenous feedback. Unlike either of the other approaches, such a strategy seeks to model a social process whose validity is based on explicit substantive considerations rather than merely on statistical adjustments for group-level errors. Of course, the endogenous feedback model is not tied to the special limiting case of equal within-"group" contiguity and zero between-"group" contiguity—more specific assumptions about social structure and interaction can and should be incorporated. Nor does the model depend on the particular kinds of exogenous variables involved—individual characteristics, group treatments, social background, or whatever. In any event, the question of whether a particular outcome such as student performance can legitimately (or plausibly) be associated with a specifiable process involving interaction among individuals and predicated on physical or social contiguity must be resolved on theoretical grounds.

CONCLUSION

Our examination of possible generating mechanisms for contextual effects has led to several interesting conclusions. We find that explicit rationalizations of the conventional model of contextual effects are either formally deficient or structually misspecified. In the former case they imply the postulation of highly implausible substantive mechanisms (e.g., "social telepathy"), while in the latter case they represent the impact of variables which are independent of social interaction altogether (e.g., common fate). Moreover, among rationalizations which do acknowledge social interaction effects, those assuming feedback among exogenous variables (e.g., group norms) merely posit contextual effects beyond the reach of estimation. Only the model based on endogenous feedback effects of social interaction (i.e., social contagion) provides a specification which is both substantively meaningful and empirically compatible with contextual explanations of social phenomena.

A natural consequence of social interaction processes is interdependence of individual outcomes. While this property is theoretically attractive it is empirically troublesome since it leads to inconsistent OLS estimators of model parameters. Fortunately, recent developments of maximum likelihood estimation in spatial lattices have provided consistent estimators for endogenous feedback models. Moreover, since the same estimation problems can be shown to arise, in the form of auto-correlated errors, whenever the investigator has omitted the relevant contextual mechanisms from the specification of the model, analogous adjustments of estimation procedure are required even with underspecified models. In particular, failure to incorporate the endogenous feedback effects of social interaction in a model of individual outcomes can be shown to entail specification bias in the form of spurious estimates of conventional "group mean" effects.

These conclusions cast serious doubt on the substantive validity of contextual models based on "group mean" effects. If the notion of contextual effects is to signify substantive rather than statistical phenomena, then the assumption that behavior begets behavior (mediated through a given social structure) has much to recommend itself. In particular, the specification of endogenous feedback allows—indeed compels—the investigator to make explicit the social interaction mechanisms believed responsible for "contextual effects" and the social contiguity structure which defines the relevant interaction opportunities. Where processes based on contiguity and interaction are not involved, the explanation of "group-level" effects, should they occur in estimation, must be sought elsewhere. Conversely, the endogenous feedback model avoids the need to postulate action at a distance through reified "group norms."

NOTES

1. Actually, b_2 would simply be proportional to $c_1 \text{Cov}(x,z)$.

2. In this case, the implied coefficient would be proportional to $p_1 p_0 b_1^*$.

3. Our model was inspired by Mitchell (1969), who uses a similar idea to treat the effects of spatial contiguity in explaining the take-over of local municipalities by guerilla insurgents in Southeast Asia. We would like to thank Howard Rosenthal for bringing this model to our attention. The model has also been discussed in Doreian and Hummon (1976: chs. 6-7).

4. The parameter α is analogous to the feedback rate in a dynamic model, but here feedback is filtered (weighted) by a two-dimensional structure ("lattice") of social ("spatial") contiguity rather than a one-dimensional structure of temporal contiguity.

5. Values of α greater than unity would imply that indirect ("filtered") effects attributable to the impact of exogenous variables on other members of the group become stronger rather than weaker with increasing "distance" (assuming that W is normalized to row sums of unity). More generally, the conditions for stability or "spatial" equilibrium are that $\alpha \text{Re}(\lambda_i) < 1$, where $\text{Re}(\lambda_i)$ is the real part of any eigenvalue λ_i of W; thus, stability requires that $\alpha < 1/\text{Re}(\lambda_{max})$ where λ_{max} is the largest eigenvalue of W (assuming $\lambda_{max} > 0$ as will be the case with most definitions of contiguity). For the special case of W row-normalized considered above, the largest eigenvalue is 1.0, and hence the stability condition is: $\alpha < 1$. Here, the endogenous feedback model is presented only in its equilibrium form, i.e., after all social-spatial spillover effects have run their course completely (the distribution of y as mediated by the structure of the social process based on W is being mapped back onto itself and is hence stable).

6. Autocorrelation is here defined in terms of a two-dimensional lattice, sometimes referred to as lattice autocorrelation or "spatial" autocorrelation.

7. Actually, W should be represented by blocks of $(\ell\ell' - I_n)/(n-1)$ since the main diagonal of W is zero by definition: for any given individual (i), interaction effects can emanate only from (all) *other* members of the group (i'). Thus the conventional "group

mean" formulation is misspecified to begin with, with the result that the parameter α is replaced by the quantity $\alpha[n/(n-1+\alpha)]$. However, we shall ignore this distortion for the purpose of the argument in this section.

8. This result can be derived as follows (for W block-diagonal, with blocks of $W_j = \ell\ell'/n$):

Let: $X_1 = [\ell \tilde{X}_1]$, where ℓ is an n by 1 vector of 1's, and $\tilde{X}_1$ is the n by $(p-1)$ matrix of observations on the regular regressors for classroom 1; and let y_1 be the n by 1 vector of observations on the dependent variable for classroom 1.

Then the "within" OLS estimator bias is given by the expectation of:

$$(X_1' X_1)^{-1} X_1' \alpha W_1 y_1 = \alpha (X_1' X_1)^{-1} X_1' W_1 y_1$$

$$= \alpha \begin{bmatrix} \ell'\ell & \ell'\tilde{X}_1 \\ \tilde{X}_1'\ell & \tilde{X}_1'\tilde{X}_1 \end{bmatrix}^{-1} \begin{bmatrix} \ell'y_1 \\ \tilde{X}_1'\left(\dfrac{\ell\ell'}{n}\right)y_1 \end{bmatrix}$$

$$= \alpha \begin{bmatrix} \left(\dfrac{1}{n}\right)\ell'y_1 \\ 0 \end{bmatrix}$$

The last step uses the formula for the inverse of a partitioned matrix given in Theil (1971: 18).

9. To extend the analysis in note 8 to a group of m classrooms, we set $W = (I \otimes \ell\ell'/n)$. For this latter definition of W the "total" OLS estimator bias is equivalent to the expectation of:

$$(X'X)^{-1} X' \alpha W y = \alpha (X'X)^{-1} X' W y$$

$$= \alpha \begin{bmatrix} \sum\limits_{j=1}^{m} \ell'\ell & \sum\limits_{j=1}^{m} \ell'\tilde{X}_j \\ \sum\limits_{j=1}^{m} \tilde{X}_j'\ell & \sum\limits_{j=1}^{m} \tilde{X}_j'\tilde{X}_j \end{bmatrix}^{-1} \begin{bmatrix} n \sum\limits_{j=1}^{m} \bar{y}_j \\ \sum\limits_{j=1}^{m} \tilde{X}_j'\bar{y}_j \end{bmatrix}$$

(where $\bar{y}_1$ is the mean value on the dependent variable for the jth classroom, and $\tilde{X}_j$ is an n by $(P-1)$ matrix of observations for the regular exogenous variables for the jth classroom).

Upon expanding the expression after the last "=" sign, it will be found that for $W = (I \otimes \ell\ell'/n)$ the terms for *both* the constant term and the slope coefficients of the regular regressors are nonzero.

10. In effect, the inclusion of a "group mean" term when estimating an individual-level model may serve as a practically useful device to reduce bias in the "individual

effect" estimates under these circumstances, even though the resulting "group effect" estimates would be meaningless or inappropriate.

APPENDIX

Contextual effects may also be embedded in the error structure of a model. For example, autocorrelated errors may represent the effects of common fate variables and/or feedback processes omitted from the specification; in particular, they may arise as a result of failing to include endogenous feedback terms in the model, as discussed in the text. These implicit contextual effects can be summarized graphically, as in Figure 7. Note that the correlations among the errors could be due to common fate variables (a), feedback among "exogenous" variables (b), or endogenous feedback (c) (as indicated in Figure 7).

In these situations, the resulting autocorrelation among the error terms will require special adjustments in order to avoid inconsistent estimators. Thus, the structural specification of the "model" of Figure 7 is given by

$$y = X\beta + u \qquad\qquad [A1]$$

where

$$u = \rho Wu + \epsilon \qquad [\epsilon \sim IID]. \qquad [A2]$$

The autocorrelated errors assumption in equation A2 can be written as

$$(I - \rho W)u = \epsilon \qquad\qquad [A3]$$

hence

$$u = (I - \rho W)^{-1}\epsilon. \qquad\qquad [A4]$$

Substituting this result back into the model (equation A1)

$$y = X\beta + (I - \rho W)^{-1}\epsilon \qquad\qquad [A5]$$

and multiplying through by $(I - \rho W)$ yields

$$(I - \rho W)y = (I - \rho W)X\beta + \epsilon. \qquad\qquad [A6]$$

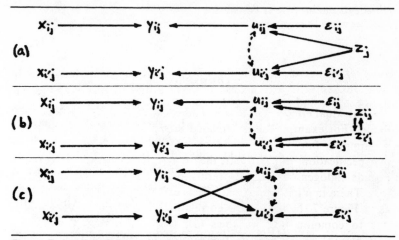

Figure 7: Implicit Context Model(s) of Correlated Errors

For ρ known, equation A6 could be estimated by OLS, using

$$Z = V\beta + \epsilon \qquad [A7]$$

where

$$Z = (I-\rho W)y \qquad [A8]$$

and

$$V = (I-\rho W)X. \qquad [A9]$$

For ρ unknown, one might consider working with the formulation

$$y = \rho y_L + X\beta - X_L\gamma + \epsilon \qquad [A10]$$

where

$$y_L = Wy \qquad [A11]$$

and

$$X_L = WX \qquad [A12]$$

subject to the nonlinear constraint

$$\gamma = \rho\beta. \qquad [A13]$$

However, it can be shown that, even with the constraint, OLS in equation A10 will yield inconsistent estimators (analogous to the case of the endogenous feedback model considered in the text). Hence an alternative approach is needed. Ord (1975) suggests an iterative procedure, using OLS in equation A6 conditional on a given estimate of ρ and using the MLE from equation 14 in equation A3 above on the residuals of equation A1, i.e., conditional on a given estimate of β from equation A6. The two-step process is repeated until convergence of parameter estimates is reached (Cochrane-Orcutt procedure), or until the residuals in equation A6 no longer reveal significant autocorrelation (Prais-Winston procedure), using a test proposed by Ord (1975). Optionally, iteration might be preceded by a simple grid search based on OLS in equation A7 to determine an approximate starting value for ρ.

The explicit or implicit specification of contextual feedback effects and the methods for estimating the parameters of such models can be extended to other, more complex situations. For example, the assumption of endogenous feedback may be appropriate on theoretical grounds (social contagion process), but in addition, similar feedback processes, or common fate effects, may also be operating with respect to unspecified exogenous factors (i.e., among the error terms of the model). This situation implies an endogenous feedback model with an autoregressive error structure, i.e.,

$$(I-\alpha W)y = X\beta + u \qquad [A14]$$

with

$$(I-\rho W)u = \epsilon \qquad [\epsilon \sim IID] \qquad [A15]$$

which leads to the second-order equation

$$(I-\rho W)(I-\alpha W)y = (I-\rho W)X\beta + \epsilon \qquad [A16]$$

or

$$(I-(\alpha+\rho)W - \alpha\rho W^2)y = (I-\rho W)X\beta + \epsilon. \qquad [A17]$$

Estimation may again be accomplished by an iterative procedure, using equation A16 to estimate α and β conditional on ρ by the MLE method detailed above, using equation A15 to estimate ρ conditional on α and β, again by MLE, and repeating the process until convergent parameter estimates or uncorrelated residuals are reached. Again, a two-dimensional grid search might serve to supply starting values for α and ρ.

Comparison of equations A5 and A6 points up a further problem which will often complicate empirical analysis. Thus, equation A5 is a structural model with an infinite "moving-average" disturbance (which can be written as a first-order autoregressive error, as in equation A1), while equation A6 is merely an estimating equation which *appears* to suggest endogenous feedback as well as "direct" contextual effects (in the sense of social telepathy) when in fact neither assumption is part of the underlying structural model. The reverse also holds, e.g., the endogenous feedback model of the previous section

$$(I-\alpha W)y = X\beta + u \qquad [A18]$$

in its reduced form

$$y = (I-\alpha W)^{-1}X\beta + (I-\alpha W)^{-1}lu \qquad [A19]$$

similarly implies an infinite "moving-average" error

$$v = (I-\alpha W)^{-1}u \qquad [A20]$$

which, in turn, could again be written as a first-order autoregressive disturbance

$$(I-\alpha W)v = u. \qquad [A21]$$

Thus, except for the structure of the exogenous term, equation A6 and A18 are empirically indistinguishable, even though they are making quite different substantive assumptions about contextual processes. Finally, equation A16 would be indistinguishable from a "genuine" second-order endogenous feedback model (to the extent that the latter assumption makes sense in a spatial or social lattice). Ultimately, as always, only prior specification on substantive grounds can guide the decision between alternative forms.

REFERENCES

ALEXANDER, N. C. and E. L. McDILL (1976) "Selection and allocation within schools: some causes and consequences of curriculum placement." Amer. Soc. Rev. 41 (December): 963-980.

ALWIN, D. F. (1976) "Assessing school effects: some identities." Sociology of Education 49 (October).

BARTON, A. H. (1970) "Allen Barton comments on Hauser's 'context and consex'." Amer. J. of Sociology 76 (November): 514-517.

――― (1968) "Bringing society back in: survey research and macro-methodology." Behavioral Scientist, 1-9.

BIDWELL, C. E. and J. D. KASARDA (1975) "School district organization and student achievement." Amer. Soc. Rev. 40 (February): 55-70.

BLAU, P. M. (1960) "Structural effects." Amer. Soc. Rev. 25 (April): 178-193.

BOUDON, R. (1967) L'Analyse Mathematique des Faits Sociaux. Paris: Plon.

CAMPBELL, E. Q. and C. N. ALEXANDER (1965) "Structural effects and interpersonal relationships." Amer. J. of Sociology 71 (November): 284-289.

COLEMAN, J. S. (1958) "Relational analysis: the study of social organization with survey methods." Human Organization 17: 28-36.

――― E. Q. CAMPBELL, C. J. HOBSON, J. McPARTLAND, A. MOOD, F. D. WEINFELD, and R. L. YORK (1966) Equality of Educational Opportunity. Washington, DC: Government Printing Office.

CRONBACH, L. J. (1976) "Research on classrooms and schools: formulation of questions, design, and analysis." Stanford, CA: Stanford Evaluation Consortium, School of Education.

DAVIS, J. A., J. L. SPAETH, and C. HUSON (1961) "A technique for analyzing the effects of group composition." Amer. Soc. Rev. 26 (April): 215-226.

DOREIAN, P. and N. P. HUMMON (1976) Modeling Social Processes. New York: Elsevier.

FARKAS, G. (1974) "Specification, residuals and contextual effects." Soc. Methods and Research 2 (November): 333-363.

HANNAN, M. T., J. H. FREEMAN, and J. W. MEYER (1976) "Specification of models for organizational effectiveness." Amer. Soc. Rev. 41 (February): 136-143.

HAUSER, R. M. (1974) "Contextual analysis revisited." Soc. Methods and Research 2 (February): 365-375.

――― (1970a) "Context and consex: a cautionary tale." Amer. J. of Sociology 75 (January): 645-664.

――― (1970b) "Hauser replies." Amer. J. of Sociology 76 (November): 517-520.

LAZARSFELD, P. F. and H. MENZEL (1969) "On the relation between individual and collective properties," pp. 499-516 in A. Etzioni (ed.) Reader on Complex Organizations. New York: Holt, Rinehart, & Winston.

McDILL, E. L., L. C. RIGSBY, and E. D. MEYERS, Jr. (1969) "Educational climates of high schools: their effects and sources." Amer. J. of Sociology 74 (May): 567-586.

MEYER, J. W. (1970) "High school effects on college intentions." Amer. J. of Sociology 76 (July): 59-70.

MITCHELL, E. J. (1969) "Some econometrics of the Huk rebellion." Amer. Pol. Sci. Rev. 63: 1159-1171.

ORD, K. (1975) "Estimation methods for models of spatial interaction." J. of the Amer. Statistical Association 70 (March): 120-126.

ROGOFF, N. (1961) "Local structure and educational selection," pp. 241-251 in A. H. Halsey, J. Floud, and C. A. Anderson (eds.) Education, Economy and Society. New York: Free Press.

THEIL, H. (1971) Principles of Econometrics. New York: John Wiley.

TURNER, R. H. (1964) The Social Context of Ambition. San Francisco: Chandler.

WERTS, C. E. and R. L. LINN (1971) "Considerations when making inferences within the analysis of covariance model." Educational and Psychological Measurement 31 (Summer): 407-416.

Lutz Erbring is Assistant Professor of Political Science and Faculty Associate in the Center for Political Studies, Institute for Social Research, at the University of Michigan. In addition to quantitative models and methods of social research, his interests include mass political behavior and international relations.

Alice A. Young is Assistant Professor in the Social Science Department at Carnegie-Mellon University. Dr. Young's research interests focus on governmental regulation and organizational theory. She is currently completing two manuscripts, To Producers and Consumers of Organizations *(with Lee Sproull) and* Federal Regulation: An Institutional Analysis.

RATIO VARIABLES IN AGGREGATE DATA ANALYSIS
Their Uses, Problems, and Alternatives

4

KENNETH A. BOLLEN
Brown University
SALLY WARD
Rutgers University

*t*he controversy over the use of ratios in correlation or regression analyses has a long history. The issue has been commented on by statisticians, sociologists, economists, political scientists, geologists, zoologists, and others (see, e.g., Pearson, 1897; Yule, 1910; Kuh and Meyer, 1955; Chayes, 1971; Schuessler, 1973; Uslaner, 1976, 1977; Atchley et al., 1976). The debate continues but it remains difficult for the nonspecialist to keep abreast of the issues involved. Social scientists are largely at a loss when it comes to guidelines to follow in actual research.

AUTHORS' NOTE: *The authors' names are listed alphabetically to represent equal contribution. K. A. Bollen is now at the General Motor Research Laboratories, Warren, MI.*

The purpose of this article is to discuss the issues that have been raised and to suggest guidelines for researchers working with ratio data.[1]

THE NATURE OF THE RATIO PROBLEM

Most of the discussions of the problem of ratio variables begin with the work of Pearson (1897, 1910). Pearson devised a formula to *approximate* the correlation between ratios that is based on the correlations (r) and coefficients of variation (V = standard deviation/mean) for the individual components:

$$r_{(y/z)(x/w)} = \frac{r_{yx}V_yV_x - r_{yw}V_yV_w - r_{xz}V_xV_z + r_{zw}V_zV_w}{\sqrt{V_y^2 + V_z^2 - 2r_{yz}V_yV_z}\ \sqrt{V_x^2 + V_w^2 - 2r_{xw}V_xV_w}} \quad [1]$$

The formula can be used for different configurations of the correlation of ratios by substitution.[2]

One of the important applications of the formula is for the correlation between ratios with a common denominator (x/z and y/z). If $r_{xy} = r_{xz} = r_{yz} = 0$ (i.e., the correlations among the components are all equal to zero), then the correlation between ratios with a common denominator (z) does *not* equal zero, but is equal to:

$$V_z^2 / \left(\sqrt{V_y^2 + V_z^2}\ \sqrt{V_x^2 + V_z^2} \right) \quad [2]$$

Pearson referred to this as a measure of "spurious correlation." The term "spurious" was used because the correlation does not result from a causal relationship between two variables but from the sharing of a common denominator.[3] Similar formulas can be derived to illustrate that the correlation between a ratio and its denominator (e.g., $r_{(x/z)z}$) will be negative when the component correlations are zero and the correlation between ratios where the denominator of one is equal to the numerator of the other (e.g., $r_{(x/z)(z/y)}$) will be negative, given the null component correlations. Pearson concluded that his approximation formulas illustrate that the interpretations of correlations between ratios are "not free from obscurity."

A number of years after Pearson's (1897) article, Yule (1910) wrote that spurious correlation does not always arise when looking at the relationship between ratio variables sharing a common element. His argument was that if the causal relationship between the variables is conceptualized in terms of ratios, then the correlation of these ratios is *not* spurious but is meaningful. Furthermore, Yule (1910: 646) argues that the correlation of two nonratio variables, x and y, may be spurious if the underlying causal relationship is between the two ratios, x/z and y/z.

The Pearson and Yule positions are most usefully applied in discussions of the theoretical nature of the relationship between the variables used in analyses. It is generally recognized that if theory suggests a relationship between two variables, x and y, and the researcher correlates ratios, say x/z and y/z, the relationship may be spurious. The main controversy is whether the correlation (or regression) involving two ratios sharing a common component leads to spurious results if the theoretical argument is presented in terms of ratios.

There is, however, an additional area of controversy that is conceptually distinct from, yet often confused with, the issue of the theoretical nature of the relationship—that of the use of ratios for control purposes. In many cases, ratios are used to control for the third variable, although the reasons for this use of ratios are often implicit. For example, studies concerned with program expenditures at the state or local level frequently use *standardized* measures of the per capita form as a dependent variable and percent variables describing population characteristics of the unit under investigation as independent variables (see, for example, Clark, 1968; Turk, 1970; Lincoln, 1976). Commonly, the use of ratios or percent measures in this context is assumed to be necessary for control purposes, but the issue is seldom raised.

A third use of ratio variables is to correct for heteroscedasticity or the unequal variances of the residuals in a regression model. In certain situations the use of ratio variables may lead to more efficient estimates of the regression coefficients than is possible using the raw components of the ratios. For example, in a study of the growth and decline of employees of educational institutions, Freeman and Hannan (1975: 223) found that the variance of the residual increased with the square of enrollment size. To correct for this unequal variance each component of the original equation was divided by enrollment size. This transformed equation corrected for heteroscedasticity by estimating an equation with ratio variables. However, not all regressions with ratio variables serve as corrections for heteroscedasticity; in fact, if the equation using the raw variables has equal residual variances then the ratio transformation will lead to unequal variances (Belsley, 1972).

In summary, there are at least three separate configurations of the ratio problem in social science research: first, the theoretical configuration where the issue is the nature of the relationship between the variables; second, the control configuration that involves the use of ratios to standardize for a third variable; and third, the use of ratios to correct for heteroscedasticity. All three uses of ratios may involve problems of inference. Each will be discussed in turn, along with suggestions for dealing with the analysis problems that may result from the use of ratios.

RATIOS AS VARIABLES
OF THEORETICAL INTEREST

One use of ratios is as measures of theoretical concepts. If we consider an index as any combination of two or more variables to measure a concept, then a ratio variable can be used as an index. The most common indices are those which are simple linear combinations of two or more variables. For example, a simple index can be formed by summing two variables (e.g., $x + z$) each of which is assumed to be linearly related to the underlying concept.

In the case of ratio variables the index is formed by dividing one variable by another (e.g., x/z) and the ratio is assumed to be linearly related to the underlying concept. The percentage of the total population living in urban areas (urban population/total population), for instance, can be used as an index of urbanization in a society. Or, the crude death rate (number of deaths/total population) can be conceptualized as an index of the mortality level in an area. Taken by *itself* there is no inherent problem with using a ratio or any other nonlinear combination of variables as an index. It is only when a ratio is correlated with another ratio both of which share a component that difficulties of interpretation can arise. Even though each ratio may be a reasonable index of a concept when considered separately, the empirical test of the relationship *between* the concepts may be obscured if the measures contain a common component.

To illustrate this problem consider two indices, I_1 and I_2:

$$I_1 = f(x,z) \qquad [3]$$
$$I_2 = f(y,z) \qquad [4]$$

I_1 is constructed as some function of x and z, and I_2 is a function of y and z. Suppose that I_1 and I_2 are simple linear functions of the variables as follows:

$$I_1 = x + z \qquad [5]$$
$$I_2 = y + z \qquad [6]$$

If the relationship between I_1 and I_2 is examined, part of the association found results from the use of z in the construction of both indices—in a sense, a relationship is built into both indices. The work of a researcher who claims to find a significant relationship between these two indices and the concepts that they represent may be criticized. The relationship found can result partially or totally as the result of the indices sharing the z variable. The indices taken by themselves may be largely valid indicators of the concept that they are intended to measure, but when the relationship between the indices is explored an artifactual relationship cannot easily be ruled out because of the common component used to construct both indices.

Although this index "contamination" problem is most commonly treated in the case of additive indices such as equations 5 and 6 the idea can be extended to the nonlinear situation of ratio variables. A ratio variable can be used to measure some concept just as the additive index is used for the same purpose. In these cases the indices formed are a nonlinear combination of two or more variables. This common nonlinear form is represented in equations 7 and 8:

$$I_1 = x/z \qquad\qquad [7]$$
$$I_2 = y/z \qquad\qquad [8]$$

In many situations z is a size variable such as population. If the relationship between I_1 and I_2 is examined, the problem of index contamination once again arises—the empirical relationship between the indices may be partially or totally a result of the common variable used in their construction. McNemar (1962: 162) has referred to this as the problem of spurious index correlation.

Contemporary research using ratio variables implicitly assumes that their use is not a problem as long as the causal relationship is viewed as holding between the ratios. However widely accepted this view may be, it is not without difficulties. Even with theoretical justification, the use of ratios in this context requires some effort on the part of the researcher to demonstrate that the resulting correlation or regression coefficient between two or more ratios is due to a causal relationship and is not simply the result of a shared component.

For instance, if a researcher is interested in the cross-national relationship between economic development and fertility, he/she may select GNP per capita (GNP/population) and the Crude Birth Rate (# births/population) as measures of development and fertility, respectively. Even though theory suggests that development is related to fertility the empirical test of this hypothesis may be affected by the common population component that is used in both measures.

In some situations it is possible to reformulate the hypothesis such that the shared component situation does not arise. Thus, in the test of the effect of economic development on fertility, the number of births can be regressed on GNP and population as two separate explanatory variables. In this fashion it is possible to evaluate the impact of GNP on the fertility level controlling for the population of a country. In addition, the effect of population on fertility controlling for GNP is also estimated. This approach can be readily applied to many situations where the ratio variables share a common component. The ratio estimates of y/z with x/z can be reformulated as y regressed on x and z. In general the regression coefficients from the ratio and the nonratio forms will differ but the second approach avoids some of the potential problems arising from ratio regressions.

However, in some situations this nonratio alternative is not readily available. An example of one such situation can be found in the work on deterrence. Logan (1972) argues that deterrence research is addressed to the relationship between the imprisonment rate (number of admissions to prison/number of crimes, A/C) and the crime rate (number of crimes/population, C/P). According to this logic, the two ratios are theoretically meaningful as ratios. This is not to argue that the inferences made from the regression of C/P on A/C are unambiguous. There are problems in teasing out the effect of the common term. It is also difficult to reformulate these measures in terms of a nonratio alternative.

Another example of a situation where a nonratio formulation is difficult to derive is in relationships dealing with population density. Stephen (1972), for example, tests the relationship between size (area) and density (population/area). Building on a theory of Durkheim's, Stephen hypothesizes and finds a negative relationship between size and density. But, this finding is somewhat unsettling given the nature of the measures used. Even if there were no relationship between area and population a negative relationship could easily result between area and population/area.

In situations where the tests of the hypotheses cannot be reformulated in terms of the component variables several alternatives exist. One such alternative is suggested by Schuessler (1973, 1974). He suggests that it is informative to analyze the correlation or regression between ratios in terms of the components from which the ratios are formed. Using Pearson's approximation formula, Schuessler demonstrates how the correlation between two ratio variables can be decomposed into the correlations and coefficients of variation of the variables that make up the ratios.

A second suggestion for checking the results of analyses with ratios may be found in the work of Chayes (1971), a geologist. Building on Pearson's original work, Chayes suggests that some analyses of ratios can be handled by comparing the correlation coefficients or regression coefficients that are derived from the actual data used in an analysis with a set of *simulated* data whose components have the same means and standard deviations as the actual data but a near-zero intercorrelation. The simulated data meet the "spuriousness" conditions described by Pearson— a zero correlation between components, but a nonzero correlation among the resulting ratios. Chayes suggests a significance test by which to test the hypothesis that the *actual* coefficients are significantly different from the *spurious* coefficients. Although this test may be useful to determine the completely spurious case, it will not aid in the situation where part of the relationship is causal and part is spurious. In social science research, this will be the most common situation—the components will not be completely uncorrelated but will be moderate to high in magnitude. For example, suppose the correlation between two ratios is found to be significantly different from the correlation that would result if there were a zero intercorrelation among all of the components. This would tell us that, at a certain level of significance, the resulting relationship is of a different magnitude than in the completely spurious situation, but it does not tell us if some part of the relationship is solely the result of the shared component.

Returning to the work of Logan (1972), we find another suggestion for a check on the spuriousness of correlation between ratios. The specific variables in Logan's analysis are crime rate (number of crimes divided by population size) and certainty of imprisonment (number of admissions to prison divided by number of crimes). The common element in these two ratios is the number of crimes, and the ratios are used for theoretical rather than control purposes. Logan suggests that despite the theoretical justification for the use of these ratios, inference problems may result from the common term. As a check on the correlation between the ratios, Logan suggests the technique of part correlation. This technique involves removing the effects of the common term from one ratio only, in this case from the certainty measure. The correlation coefficients obtained in this way are then compared to the simple coefficient obtained by correlating the two ratios. If significant coefficients are obtained even with the control allowed by part correlation, then it can be concluded that the relation between the ratios is not spurious; i.e., it is not a result of the simultaneous effects of the common term on each ratio.

According to Fuguitt and Lieberson (1974), Logan's suggestion is related to solutions proposed by Pearson (1910), Brown et al. (1914), Neifeld (1927), and Fleiss and Tanur (1971). Fuguitt and Lieberson discuss the Logan solution and conclude that more work is necessary on the rationale for part or partial correlations before this approach is adopted as an unambiguous solution. The essential problem appears to be the same as that discussed above with reference to Chayes' work. We know from the work of Pearson what to expect when the correlations among all components of the ratio measures are equal to zero. The Pearson approximation formula provides us with the tool to predict the extent of spuriousness under this null assumption. (Chayes' work also provides such a tool.) However, in social science research the component correlations frequently depart from the null assumption. Although Logan's work was formulated to deal with the situation where the independence assumption is unreasonable (i.e., there is a nonzero correlation between number of crimes and population size), the statistical rationale for the Logan approach (see Fleiss and Tanur, 1971) involves the independence assumption.

In summary, where ratios are used for theoretical reasons, it may be premature to dismiss entirely the spuriousness issue. In research problems of this sort, it is wise to examine the data carefully according to the various suggestions from the literature on ratio correlations, the most common of which have been reviewed here.

RATIOS AS METHODS OF CONTROL

As we have argued above, in many cases ratios are used in social science research to standardize measures for some commonly operating third variable, frequently population size. This method of control (standardization or "deflation") is usually implicit; rarely are discussions given for the rationale behind this use of ratios. The problem with this use of ratios is clear and generally recognized; if the interest lies in the relationship between two component variables, x and y, that are both related to a third variable, z, x and y are frequently deflated or standardized for z through the creation of ratios, x/z and y/z. However, it has been shown (Kuh and Meyer, 1955) that only under special conditions is the correlation between the ratios ($r_{(x/z)\ (y/z)}$) equal to the partial correlation ($r_{yx \cdot z}$), and thus "one would seldom be justified in using the former as a substitute for the latter" (Fuguitt and Lieberson, 1974: 138). It follows that if one is interested in the relationship between the components, x and y, the use of ratios where z is the common denominator (or deflator) can yield misleading results.

One alternative to using ratios for control purposes is to use residualizing techniques (Pendleton et al., 1978; Schuessler, 1974; Fuguitt and Lieberson, 1974; Freeman and Kronenfeld, 1973). Vanderbok (1977: 182) suggests regressing the variables of interest on the deflating third variable and examining the relationship between the residuals. So instead of using the ratios y/z and x/z, the residuals from the regression of y on z (say, $e_{y\cdot z}$) and x on z ($e_{x\cdot z}$) are generated. The residuals, $e_{y\cdot z}$ and $e_{x\cdot z}$, are uncorrelated with z and can be used as new variables in a second regression of $e_{y\cdot z}$ on $e_{x\cdot z}$.

Although this residual approach seems intuitively appealing, several factors should be kept in mind. First, the regression coefficient(s) from the regression of the ratio variables is rarely equal to the regression coefficient(s) from the residual regressions (Schuessler, 1974: 395). That is, the regression coefficient of y/z regressed on x/z usually differs from the regression coefficient of $e_{y\cdot z}$ on $e_{x\cdot z}$. It is conceivable that the regression coefficient from the ratio regression may be significant while the residual regression is not, or vice versa. This is not unexpected, since the argument concerning ratios is that their use may lead to biased estimates.

A second point to keep in mind is that there is a close relationship between the residual approach and the "component" approach. Instead of using the regression of $e_{y\cdot z}$ on $e_{x\cdot z}$, the component approach uses the regression of y on x *and* z, all in one step. Thus, in the component approach, the deflating variable is entered as an additional explanatory variable. Interestingly enough, the regression coefficient for x in the component approach is *exactly equal* to the regression coefficient for $e_{x\cdot z}$ in the residual approach. However, the standard errors of the regression coefficients, which are used to evaluate the significance of the coefficients, are likely to be different.

The standard errors of the regression coefficients for the residual and the component approach may differ for three reasons: (1) differences in explained variances; (2) differences in the variance of the explanatory variable; and (3) differences in the intercorrelation of explanatory variables.[4] The explained variances or R^2s in the residual and component approaches are rarely the same, because each regression has a different dependent variable; $e_{y\cdot z}$ in the residual case and y in the component case. In fact, the correlation resulting from the residual regression is equivalent to the partial correlation coefficient of y with x, controlling for z ($r_{yx \cdot z}$). This partial correlation coefficient is usually less than the multiple correlation coefficient of y on x and z. Since the contribution of z to y (and to x) is likely to be large (otherwise there is little need to control for z by any of the mechanisms discussed here), the total variance explained will usually be much smaller for the residualized case than for the component case.

A second determinant of the standard error is the variance of the explanatory variable in a regression. The residual and component regression are likely to have different variation in the explanatory variable, since different explanatory variables are used: $e_{x \cdot z}$ in the residual case and x in the component case. Finally, the intercorrelation of the explanatory variables also differs. In the case of the residual example, there is only one explanatory variable, $e_{x \cdot z}$, so there is no intercorrelation, thereby reducing the standard error. In the component approach, the intercorrelation between x and z must be considered; the greater the correlation, the greater the standard error.

It would be quite surprising if these three contributions to the standard error balanced out so that the standard errors in the residual and component approaches were equal. Therefore, although the regression coefficients for $e_{x \cdot z}$ in the residualized approach and x in the component approach are identical, they are not likely to have the same estimated standard errors. The significance of x may thus depend on whether the residual or component approach is used; clearly an ambiguous situation.

An argument can be made that the estimated standard error for the residual approach is misleading since it represents a two-stage procedure and each stage involves sampling error. In the first stage, the variables y and x are regressed separately on a third variable, z. Clearly there will be different residuals estimated depending on the sample that is used. This sampling fluctuation in the estimated residuals should be kept in mind when examining the second stage where the residuals are regressed on one another. Since the regression coefficient is the same in the component and residual approach, and the component approach involves only one stage, the component approach may actually be more desirable than the residual approach, depending on the particular research problem at hand.

The component alternative to using ratios as control variables parallels an alternative to ratio variables discussed in the last section. When ratios are used as a measure of a concept or for control purposes, it may be possible to reformulate the analysis in terms of the component variables rather than the ratio variables. If GNP per capita is treated as an indicator of economic development, it is possible to consider GNP controlling population as an alternative measure of economic development. Or, if GNP per capita is used to control the effects of population on GNP, it is possible to reformulate the analysis to examine the effects of GNP controlling population as an additional explanatory variable.

One potential problem with this component approach is that if x and z are closely related, multicollinearity may make it difficult to accurately assess the separate effects of x and z on the dependent variable, y. It remains an empirical question as to how serious a problem this will be in practice. The problem of multicollinearity is commonly found in many areas of study in the social sciences. This case, if it arises, should be treated like any other: if possible, bring new data or information to the problem to help increase the efficiency of the estimates (Farrar and Glauber, 1967); use a procedure such as ridge regression (Hoerl and Kennard, 1970; Marquardt and Snee, 1975; Feig, 1978); or drop variables from the analysis that contribute only marginally. The treatment of multicollinearity is beyond the scope of this article, but the reader can consult a number of sources for a discussion of this problem (see, for example, Johnston, 1972; Goldberger, 1964; Rockwell, 1975). In addition, the problem of multicollinearity may arise in ratio models (see, for example, Deegan, 1975), so it is not unique to the component approach.

In summary, it is unlikely that ratios will be adequate control devices. If the researcher is interested in explicitly controlling the effects of a variable, it is often better to enter the variable as an additional explanatory variable in the regression equation.

RATIOS AS A CORRECTION
FOR HETEROSCEDASTICITY

A third use of ratio variables is to correct for heteroscedasticity. Heteroscedasticity exists when the variances of the errors from a regression equation are not constant. The consequences of heteroscedasticity are that the Ordinary Least Square (OLS) estimates of the regression coefficients are unbiased and consistent but not efficient (Kmenta, 1971: 254). Thus, the estimates have some desirable properties, but the lack of constant variance biases the computed standard errors of the regression coefficients; this causes problems with the standard tests of significance.

The usual regression equation with component or "undeflated" variables is:

$$Y = \alpha_o + \alpha_1 Z + \alpha_2 X + \epsilon \qquad [9]$$

However, as Kuh and Meyer (1955: 406) have pointed out: "with undeflated cross-section data the assumption of constant error variance usually is not appropriate." A Weighted Least Squares (WLS) model is commonly suggested in econometrics literature as an alternative to OLS when the error variances are not equal. If the residual variance in equation 9 is proportional to the square of Z, the appropriate WLS model can be found by multiplying both sides of equation 9 by $1/Z$:

$$Y/Z = \alpha_o(1/Z) + \alpha_1 + \alpha_2(X/Z) + \epsilon/Z \qquad [10]$$

Equation 10 is a Weighted Least Squares form of equation 9 which will yield constant variance of the residuals, *providing* that the residual variance of 9 has been correctly identified as being proportional to Z^2. If this specification is correct, the WLS model will correct for heteroscedasticity and will estimate more efficiently the parameters of equation 9.

Note that the WLS model of equation 10 leads to a different equation than the usual ratio equation:

$$Y/Z = \alpha_1 + \alpha_2(X/Z) + \mu \qquad [11]$$

Equations 10 and 11 differ in that equation 10 has $1/Z$ as an additional variable on the right-hand side of the equation. The researcher will get different results depending on which equation is estimated; equation 11 may yield biased results due to the omitted variable if the model that should be estimated is equation 10 (Belsley, 1972).

The reason for this difference becomes clear if we "undeflate" equation 11 by multiplying each side of the equation by Z:

$$Y = \alpha_1 Z + \alpha_2 X + \mu Z \qquad [12]$$

Note that this equation differs from the components equation (9) presented at the beginning of this discussion; equation 9 contains a constant term, while equation 12 does not. If the model to be specified contains a constant and can be appropriately weighted with $1/Z$, then the usual ratio model (11) is not the appropriate model to be estimated.

Furthermore, suppose that the residual variance of equation 9 is not proportional to Z^2, but to Z. In this case, the WLS model to be estimated is:

$$Y/\sqrt{Z} = \alpha_0 (1/\sqrt{Z}) + \alpha_1(\sqrt{Z}) + \alpha_2(X/\sqrt{Z}) + \epsilon/\sqrt{Z} \qquad [13]$$

Compare this to the usual ratio model (equation 11), and the differences are once again obvious.

From the above, we can conclude that the usual ratio variable equation, $Y/Z = \alpha_1 + \alpha_2 X/Z + \mu$ can *only* be justified as a correction for heteroscedasticity under the following two conditions; (1) the original equation does not have a constant term, and (2) the variances of the residuals of the original equation are proportional to Z^2. In short the original equation is $Y = \alpha_1 Z + \alpha_2 X + \mu Z$.

Neither of these criteria should be taken lightly. If the researcher believes that the original equation does contain a constant term, then the usual ratio equation (11) is not appropriate. Similarly, there are many different forms that heteroscedastic errors can assume. Assuming that the error variance is proportional to Z^2 is one possibility of many. For example, the error variance may be proportional to Z, some other variable, or to the predicted value of the dependent variable. In any of these cases the WLS transformed equation does not use 1/Z but some other weight. In addition, in many situations heteroscedasticity can be corrected by estimating the equation with all or some of the variables logarithmically transformed. The choice of using log transformed variables depends upon other characteristics such as the skewness of the original variables, whether the relationship is nonlinear, and so on, but logs should be considered as an alternative.[5]

The overriding point we wish to make is that ratio variables are *not* a universal solution to heteroscedasticity. The original form of the equation and the nature of the heteroscedasticity determine the nature of the transformed equation required.

SUMMARY

The purpose of this article, as stated at the outset, was to provide an overview of issues that have been raised over the use of ratios in correlation and regression analyses *and* to suggest guidelines for researchers working with ratio data. In meeting the first of these purposes, the technical problems with ratios and alternatives to ratios have been discussed; we would like to return now to our second purpose of providing guidelines for researchers working with ratio data and summarize by suggesting several alternatives. Our major argument here is that the indiscriminate use of ratios should be avoided. The best research strategy may well be the use of multiple techniques as a check on findings. Any ambiguous or contradictory findings can then be reported and an attempt made to explain them.

In our search for alternatives, we have not uncovered a universal "solution" to the problem of ratio variables. The various alternatives that we have discussed are characterized by problems of their own which may cloud interpretations; but, again, we would like to stress that the lack of unambiguous alternatives is not sufficient justification for the continued use of ratio variables. Alternatives to the use of ratios correspond to the rationale for the use of ratios in the first place, as outlined above. The alternatives that seem promising are listed below.

RATIOS AS VARIABLES OF THEORETICAL INTEREST

(1) If possible, reformulate the research problem in terms of nonratio variables.

(2) If it is not possible to reformulate the problem in terms of nonratio variables, there are at least three alternatives.

    (a) Use approximation formulas to analyze relationships among components and how they contribute to relationships among ratios (see, for example, Schuessler, 1973, 1974).

    (b) Generate random variables with the same means and standard deviations as component variables but with zero correlation. The random variables can then be converted to ratios, intercorrelated, and used as a yardstick of spuriousness against which to compare the results using real ratio data. If the differences are significant, then greater confidence can be placed in the inferences drawn from the real ratio data (see, for example, Chayes, 1971).

    (c) Use part correlation (see, for example, Logan, 1972; Fuguitt and Lieberson, 1973).

ALTERNATIVES TO RATIOS AS METHODS OF CONTROL

(1) Use the components of ratios with the "standardizing" or "deflating" vaiable explicitly entered as an additional explanatory variable.

(2) Use residualizing techniques to statistically remove the effects of the "deflating" variable.

ALTERNATIVES TO RATIOS AS CORRECTION
FOR HETEROSCEDASTICITY

(1) Determine the original form of the model.

(2) Determine the nature of the heteroscedasticity.

(3) Follow the usual corrective procedures (see, for example, Kmenta, 1971).

The appropriate selection from these alternatives will depend on the research problem at hand. Given the problems associated with each of these alternatives that we have discussed in the article, sole reliance on any one alternative may be premature. In short, there is very little to lose and a great deal to gain by comparing the results from a number of alternatives before making inferences about the social processes under investigation in a particular research problem. At a minimum, such a comparative approach to data analysis will increase the certainty that parameter estimates reflect "real" social processes rather than statistical artifact.

NOTES

1. We are assuming throughout this article that the use of ratio-type variables *may* cause data analysis and inference problems. This assumption has been questioned in the literature on ratios, however. For example, the debate between Uslaner (1976, 1977) and Lyons (1977) is concerned with whether or not there *is* a problem with the correlation or regression of ratios. Rather than furthering the discussion over the existence of the problem, we feel it is more productive at this point to accept the *possibility* of problems in data analysis using ratios and to pursue methods for dealing with the problem.

2. The formula is an approximation which is most accurate when the coefficient of variation is small.

3. For a discussion of the meaning of "causal relationship" as applied in the social sciences, see Simon (1957), Blalock (1964) and Alker (1966).

4. An additional factor which may affect the standard errors is possible differences in heteroscedasticity which may vary in the component versus residual approach. This possibility is not discussed here but deserves further research.

5. If the original relationship between variables is linear, log transformations may not be appropriate since the resulting relationship is nonlinear.

REFERENCES

ALKER, H. R., Jr. (1966) "Causal inferences and political analysis," in J. Bernd (ed.) Mathematical Applications in Political Science. Dallas: Southern Methodist Univ. Press.

ATCHLEY, W., C. GASKINS, and D. ANDERSON (1976) "Statistical properties of ratios. I. Empirical results." Systematic Zoology 25: 137-148.

BELSLEY, D. (1972) "Specification with deflated variables and specious spurious correlation." Econometrica 40: 923-927.

BLALOCK, H. (1964) Causal Inferences in Nonexperimental Research. New York: W. W. Norton.

BROWN, J. W., M. GREENWOOD, Jr. and F. WOOD (1914) "A study of index correlations." J. of the Royal Statistical Society 77: 317-347.

CHAYES, F. (1971) Ratio correlation. Chicago: Univ. of Chicago Press.

CLARK, T. (1968) "Community structure, decision-making, budget expenditures, and urban renewal in 51 communities." Amer. Soc. Rev. 33: 576-593.

DEEGAN, J., Jr. (1975) "The process of political development." Soc. Methods and Research 3: 384-415.

FARRAR, D. E. and R. R. GLAUBER (1967) "Multicollinearity in regression analysis: the problem revisited." Rev. of Economics and Statistics 49: 92-107.

FEIG, D. (1978) "Ridge regression: when biased estimation is better." Social Sci. Q. 58: 708-716.

FLEISS, J. and J. TANUR (1971) "A note on the partial correlation coefficient." Amer. Statistician 25: 43-45.

FREEMAN, J. and M. T. HANNAN (1975) "Growth and decline processes in organizations." Amer. Soc. Rev. 40: 215-228.

FREEMAN, J. and J. E. KRONENFELD (1973) "Problems of definitional dependence: the case of administrative intensity." Social Forces 52: 108-121.

FUGUITT, G. and S. LIEBERSON 91974) "Correlation of ratios or difference scores having common terms," pp. 128-144 in H. Costner (ed.) Sociological Methodology 1973-1974. San Francisco: Jossey-Bass.

GOLDBERGER, A. S. (1964) Econometric Theory. New York: John Wiley.

HOERL, A. E. and R. W. KENNARD (1970) "Ridge regression: applications to non-orthogonal problems." Technometrics 12: 69-82.

JOHNSTON, J. (1972) Econometric Methods. New York: McGraw-Hill.

KMENTA, J. (1971) Elements of Econometrics. New York: Macmillan.

KUH, E. and J. R. MEYER (1955) "Correlation and regression estimates when the data are ratios." Econometrica 23: 400-416.

KUNREUTHER, H. (1966) "The use of the Pearsonian approximation in comparing deflated and undeflated regression estimates." Econometrica 34: 323-334.

LINCOLN, J. (1976) "Power mobilization in the urban community: reconsidering the ecological approach." Amer. Soc. Rev. 41: 1-15.

LOGAN, C. (1972) "General deterrent effects of imprisonment." Social Forces 51: 64-73.

LYONS, W. (1977) "Per capita index construction: a defense." Amer. J. of Pol. Sci. 21: 177-191.

MANDANSKY, A (1964) "Spurious correlation due to deflating variables." Econometrica 32: 652-655.

MARQUARDT, D. and R. SNEE (1975) "Ridge regression in practice." Amer. Statistician 29: 3-20.

McNEMAR, Q. (1962) Psychological Statistics. New York: John Wiley.

NEIFELD, M. R. (1927) "A study of spurious correlation." J. of the Amer. Statistical Association 22: 331-338.

PEARSON, K. (1910) "On the correlation of death rates." J. of the Royal Statistical Society 73: 534-539.

——— (1897) "On a form of spurious correlation which may arise when indices are used in the measurement of organs." Proceedings of the Royal Society of London 60: 489-498.

PENDLETON, B., R. WARREN, and H. C. CHANG (1978) "The problem of correlated denominators in multiple regression and change analyses." Journal Paper No. J-9127 of the Iowa Agriculture and Home Economics Experiment Station, Ames.

PRZEWORSKI, A. and F. CORTES (1977) "Comparing partial and ratio regression models." Pol. Methodology 4: 63-75.

RANGARAJAN, C. and S. CHATTERJEE (1969) "A note on comparison between correlation coefficients of original and transformed variables." Amer. Statistician 23: 28-29.

ROCKWELL, R. C. (1975) "Assessment of multicollinearity: the Haitovsky test of the determinant." Soc. Methods and Research 3: 308-320.

SCHUESSLER, K. (1974) "Analysis of ratio variables: opportunities and pitfalls." Amer. J. of Sociology 80: 379-396.

——— (1973) "Ratio variables and path models," pp. 201-228 in A. Goldberger and O. D. Duncan (eds.) Structural Equation Models in the Social Sciences. New York: Seminar.

SIMON, H. (1957) Models of Man. New York: John Wiley.

STEPHAN, G. E. (1972) "International tests of the size-density hypothesis." Amer. Soc. Rev. 37: 365-368.

TURK, H. (1970) "Interorganizational networks in urban society: initial perspective and comparative research." Amer. Soc. Rev. 35: 1-19.

USLANER, E. (1977) "Straight lines and straight thinking: can all of those econometricians be wrong?" Amer. J. of Pol. Sci. 21: 183-191.

——— (1976) "The pitfalls of per capita." Amer. J. of Pol. Sci. 20: 125-133.

VANDERBOK, W. (1977) "On improving the analysis of ratio data." Pol. Methodology 4: 171-184.

YULE, G. U. (1910) "On the interpretation of correlations between indices or ratios." J. of the Royal Statistical Society 73: 644-647.

This reference section includes all of the references cited in this article as well as additional references which we have found helpful for understanding problems associated with the use of ratios.

Kenneth A. Bollen is Associate Senior Research Scientist in the Societal Analysis Department of General Motors Research Laboratories. His areas of research are international development and statistical methodology.

Sally Ward is Assistant Professor of Sociology in the Department of Sociology, Rutgers University, Newark. She is currently involved in research on policy outputs, patterns of economic ownership, and income inequality in U.S. communities.

CORRELATED DENOMINATORS IN MULTIPLE REGRESSION AND CHANGE ANALYSES

5

BRIAN F. PENDLETON
University of Akron
RICHARD D. WARREN
H. C. CHANG
Iowa State University

Sociological and demographic research often uses variables computed as ratios or rates. Usually, the denominator of the ratio is used for control purposes, as when population size is used in the calculation of per capita income or the birthrate (Schuessler, 1974). When two ratios with highly correlated, or the same, denominators are correlated, a statistical depend-

AUTHORS' NOTE: *This is Journal Paper No. J-9127 of the Iowa Agriculture and Home Economics Experiment Station, Ames (Project No. 2146). This study is a contributing project to the North Central Regional Project NC-97, "Population Redistribution in the North Central Region—pre- and post-1970."*

ency is introduced through the shared denominator. When ratios with highly correlated denominators are used in correlation, regression, and path analyses, the calculated coefficients are influenced by the common elements in the denominators, which can lead to serious misinterpretations. This problem may be present in either cross-sectional or longitudinal research.

This article has two major purposes. First is to review problems with analysis procedure and inferences when ratios are computed by using the same or highly correlated denominators. Reasons that sociologists and demographers have not widely acknowledged this problem are posited. A description of the problem is then extended from bivariate correlation and regression to partial correlation and multiple regression. The use of residual analysis is then discussed as one solution to this problem, especially applicable when ratios' denominators are not identical.

The second purpose of this article is to expand the problem of correlated denominators from cross-sectional to longitudinal or change-analysis research. First, three techniques for measuring change are discussed: difference scores, proportions or percentages, and residualized difference scores. Discussion then focuses on path analysis as change analysis. A recently developed procedure for fitting the time order of variables into a path analytic framework is reviewed and the problem of correlated denominators in longitudinal path analysis is discussed. The reader is alerted to a probable problem with correlated denominators in all change analyses. Again, the use of residual analysis is seen as one solution for overcoming the problem of correlated denominators in longitudinal path analysis.

RATIO VARIABLES AND THE PROBLEM OF CORRELATED DENOMINATORS

This section briefly reviews the problem of correlated denominators for variables expressed as ratios or rates.[1] Two situations are introduced, one in which the ratios' denominators are the same, a second where denominators are not identical but highly correlated. For example, let $d = a/c$, $e = b/c$, and $e' = f/g$, where

$r_{cc} = 1.0$ and $r_{cg} \neq 1.0$ but the correlation is high. The denominator deflates or weights the numerator to the scale of a particular unit of analysis (Kerlinger, 1973: 151; Loether and McTavish, 1976). When describing characteristics of a phenomenon, the presentation of ratios is a valid and meaningful procedure. However, when one ratio is statistically compared with another ratio and both have the same denominators (e.g., r_{de}), the resulting association may be deceiving, regardless of whether it is expressed as a measure of association or causal influence (Vanderbok, 1977; Fuguitt and Lieberson, 1974; Schuessler, 1974). Statistically, the magnitude of the mutual dependence of a and b on c determines the spuriousness between ratios d and e. Similarly, when two ratios are statistically compared and they have different yet highly correlated denominators (e.g., $r_{de'}$), the resulting association also may be spurious (Rangarajan and Chatterjee, 1969; Schuessler, 1973; Fuguitt and Lieberson, 1974; Pendleton, 1977). Obviously, there is no problem when the correlation between denominators is low.

The problem of correlating ratios was first debated at the turn of the century by Pearson (1897, 1910) and Yule (1910) and most recently has been called to the attention of sociologists and demographers by Freeman and Kronenfeld (1973), Schuessler (1973, 1974), and Fuguitt and Lieberson (1974). All agree that correlated denominators present a difficulty, but the problem and solutions remain ambiguous.[2] Perhaps for this reason sociologists and demographers have avoided correction factors for correlated denominators. Even in the study of bivariate relationships, the transformation of ratios into logarithms (O'Connor, 1977; Schuessler, 1973, 1974), or the use of partial correlation (Kuh and Meyer, 1955; Przeworski and Cortes, 1977; Schuessler, 1973) or part correlation (Logan, 1971, 1972) becomes a complicated process. When placed into multivariate models that more accurately reflect the complexities of social and demographic processes, the consistent use of logarithms, partial correlation, or part correlation becomes an exceedingly demanding task (Freeman and Kronenfeld, 1973; Schuessler, 1974). In addition, especially when using logarithms, the interpretation of transformed variables may be quite different from what is intended by the original variables (Schuessler, 1973). The use of partial and part correlations to remove the effect of correlated denominators is still under debate (Kuh and Meyer, 1955; Madansky, 1964; Fuguitt and Lieberson, 1974). Calculation of second-order and higher partials in a multivariate framework again becomes an exceedingly demanding task and can approach the uninterpretable. The introduction of control variables in a partialling framework also requires theoretical justification, a context difficult to conceptualize for second-order and higher partials (Gordon, 1968).

Another reason that the use of ratios in more sophisticated statistical analyses has not undergone closer scrutiny lies in their traditional use in sociological and demographic work. Ratios have always made good sense descriptively; they are easy to compute and understand. The simple control provided by ratios for a major intervening variable (such as population) enhanced the use of ratios for *descriptive* purposes. Until only the past few decades, most research descriptively presented data (e.g., means, standard deviations, cross-tabulation, and rank-order procedures). The traditional ease with which ratios have been understood and computed would understandably lead few to question their use in more sophisticated statistical analyses. Recent and growing interest on the problem of correlated denominators has led sociologists to reexamine and comment on contemporary studies using ratio correlations (e.g., Freeman and Kronenfeld, 1973; Schuessler, 1973; Blalock, 1971; Duncan, 1966; Tittle, 1969; Chiricos and Waldo, 1970; Logan, 1971; Bailey, Gray and Martin, 1971). Surprisingly, demographers have uniformly avoided the issue.

Even though the multifaceted problem of correlated denominators is somewhat ambiguous, it is a situation that must be coped with in future research, sociological and especially demographic.

PARTIALS AND MULTIPLE-PARTIALS IN RATIO ANALYSES

Almost no work has been done, outside of a very few statistical theory and mathematical studies, on a partial correlation solution to ratio correlation (a notable exception is Chayes's work for petrologists and geochemists). Recall two of the variables used earlier: $d = a/c$ and $e = b/c$.

In the bivariate study of two ratio variables, economists Kuh and Meyer (1955) note that $r_{ab.c}$ is equal to r_{de} under certain circumstances. If V_c (i.e., coefficient of variation for c, the ratio of the standard deviation to the mean) $= r_{ac}V_a = r_{bc}V_b$, then $r_{de} \neq r_{ab.c}$.

The equation stating the relationship between the two ratio variables d and e, is

$$r_{de} = \frac{r_{ab}V_aV_b - r_{ac}V_aV_c - r_{bc}V_bV_c + V_c^2}{\sqrt{V_a^2 + V_c^2 - 2r_{ac}V_aV_c}\sqrt{V_b^2 + V_c^2 - 2r_{bc}V_bV_c}} \quad [1]$$

Without restating the algebraic argument (see Kuh and Meyer, 1955: 404-405), we note simply that, given $V_c = r_{ac}V_a = r_{bc}V_b$ (i.e., variables a and b are *each* linear homogeneous functions of c):

$$r_{de} = \frac{r_{ab}V_aV_b - V_c^2}{\sqrt{V_a^2 - V_c^2}\sqrt{V_b^2 - V_c^2}} = \frac{r_{ab} - r_{ac}r_{bc}}{\sqrt{1.0 - r_{ac}^2}\sqrt{1.0 - r_{bc}^2}} = r_{ab.c} \quad [2]$$

Necessary and sufficient conditions for r_{de} and $r_{ab.c}$ to approach equality and for r_{de} to be at its lowest with respect to V_c are (Kuh and Meyer, 1955: 405): (1) that V_c be small and (2) that the variables undergoing control or deflation each are linear homogeneous functions of the correlated denominators. At any other time, when $V_c \neq r_{ac}V_a \neq r_{bc}V_b$, r_{de} will be greater than $r_{ab.c}$. This is an expected consequence because the ratio correlation, imbued with the shared effects of a common denominator, will have a value higher than a partial correlation between the two numerators with the influence of shared denominators held constant. Again, only magnitude is referred to here; the direction of the relationship may be positive or negative (Rangarajan and Chatterjee, 1969).

The discussion on the bivariate study of two ratio variables may be extended to multivariate analysis where one deals with more than two ratio variables and multiple regression may be thought of as a series of partial correlations. To show that the bivariate case is generalizable to the multivariate case let $h = i/c$. Continuing with the same assumptions as before (i.e., V_c is small, and the variables a, b, and i are each linear homogeneous functions of c), we have:

$$r_{ab.ci} = \frac{r_{ab.c} - r_{ai.c}r_{bi.c}}{\sqrt{1.0 - r_{ai.c}^2}\sqrt{1.0 - r_{bi.c}^2}} = \frac{r_{de} - r_{dh}r_{eh}}{\sqrt{1.0 - r_{dh}^2}\sqrt{1.0 - r_{eh}^2}} = r_{de.h} \quad [3]$$

where

$$r_{de} = r_{ab.c} \text{ (from the bivariate case)}$$
$$r_{dh} = r_{ai.c} \text{ (from the bivariate case)}$$
$$r_{eh} = r_{bi.c} \text{ (from the bivariate case)}$$

and,

$$r_{ab.c} = \frac{r_{ab} - r_{ac}r_{bc}}{\sqrt{1.0 - r_{ac}^2}\sqrt{1.0 - r_{bc}^2}}$$

$$r_{ai.c} = \frac{r_{ai} - r_{ac}r_{ic}}{\sqrt{1.0 - r_{ac}^2}\sqrt{1.0 - r_{ic}^2}}$$

$$r_{bi.c} = \frac{r_{bi} - r_{bc}r_{ic}}{\sqrt{1.0 - r_{bc}^2}\sqrt{1.0 - r_{ic}^2}}$$

It follows, therefore, *that the multiple correlation coefficient calculated with ratio variables is equal to the multiple correlation calculated with, in our case, numerators that have the common denominator partialed out.* The logical extension of this conclusion leads to Freeman and Kronenfeld's (1973: 117) suggestion that "referring to the A/P ratio, we can regress A on P and look for correlates of the residuals." This is the same as DuBois' (1957) view that ratios are a special case of residuals. If, in the case of a multivariate model, each ratio variable is expressed as a residual in which the numerator has been regressed on the denominator, we have a multivariate model of residuals that should have final values similar to those in a multivariate model consisting of ratio variables. This assumes small coefficients of variation for correlated denominators and linear homogeneous functions between variables, or, for the latter case, operating with assumptions similar to any least-squares analysis. Violation of the assumptions for the ratio variable-residual variable approaches to constructing multivariate models would almost certainly lead to discrepancies when comparing the approaches. We note also that, unlike ratio variables, residuals are not directly interpretable in a descriptive sense. Deviations from linear regression for a particular variable are not directly comparable to the ratio value of the same variable (Schuessler, 1974). However, values calculated from either ratio variables or residualized variables (e.g., path coefficients) should, within a margin of error, be similar.

The researcher usually constructs a ratio to control for the effect of a variable. The nature of social science data does not allow for the more exact control achievable in experimental designs in which subjects are manipulable; control must be accomplished statistically through ratio formation, part and partial correlation, regression approaches, analysis of variance and covariance, and so on. One difficulty with all methods of statistical control is an exact interpretation of the standardized results; residual analysis is no different. Residual analysis is another method of control, but suggested specifically for use with correlated denominators. If, for example, one has a multivariate model constructed with ratios that have the same denominator, a standard least-squares regression approach in which the common denominator is entered first as a control variable, before the different numerators are entered as independent variables, may be most appropriate (Freeman and Kronenfeld, 1973). Or, if one has a multivariate model constructed with ratios that have correlated, but not necessarily the same, denominators, the computation of new variables consisting of residualized values (i.e., each variable's numerator regressed on the denominator) may be most appropriate. Although these approaches are not free of problems (Freeman and Kronenfeld, 1973: 117-119), they seem to provide results that are more manageable and far less spurious and misleading than those produced with correlated denominators.

The discussion in the next section centers on the evaluation of three techniques for measuring change between two points in time. A method of change analysis and interpretation particularly well suited for path analysis is reviewed and discussed. Then the problem of correlated denominators is applied to this method, and a solution using residuals is suggested.

THE MEASUREMENT AND ANALYSIS OF CHANGE

The analysis and intepretation of longitudinal relationships differs significantly from the study of cross-sectional relationships. In cross-sectional studies, independent samples are drawn at the same point in time. Longitudinal studies sample the same unit of analysis at two or more points in time (Baltes, 1968; Lord, 1963).

Attempts by behavioral scientists to measure change over time in a particular phenomenon range from simple observation, or the "eyeballing" of data at successive points in time, to sophisticated and complicated trend analyses. In no instance, however, is a particular technique for evaluating change met with approval by everyone. Quite literally, the measurement of change and the formation of longitudinal designs open a "Pandora's Box" of dispute and controversy. Although the various techniques have certain advantages, there also are limitations. Nevertheless, there is widespread agreement that longitudinal methodologies in sociology and demography are necessary and used increasingly in social science research (Loether and McTavish, 1976: 584-585; Social Science Research Council, 1976, 1977; Harris, 1963).

Because of the nature of demographic research, data sets often are ordered through time. Longitudinal analyses in demography generally have been of two types (Schubnell and Herberger, 1973): (1) trend observations for a particular set of data expressed in graph or tabular form in which changes in the flow of data are evaluated nonstatistically, and (2) hypothetical constructs of data as in life table or generational analyses (U.S. Bureau of the Census, 1975).

THE MEASUREMENT OF CHANGE

Reviewed now are three selected approaches to measuring change. First is the difference score, which is simply the difference in a variable at two points in time and is defined as:

$$d_x = x_2 - x_1 \qquad [4]$$

where

x_1 = value of variable x at time 1.
x_2 = value of variable x at time 2.

Although the absolute value of the difference score can be used for certain research purposes, most differences scores retain a positive or negative direction. The difference score is perhaps the most "common-sensical" approach to measuring change (Goldfarb, 1960) and has been used extensively both in descriptive research (Barclay, 1958) and in statistical analyses. It is computationally simple, easy to understand and explain, and descriptively makes good sense. Many times it is desirable to evaluate how a variable at time 1 is related to change in another variable between time 1 and time 2, or how change between time 1 and time 2 is related to the "situation" of another variable at time 2. This often is done to assess how antecedent conditions relate to change variables or how change affects a later situation. When change between time 1 and time 2 is calculated as a difference score, its correlation with time 1 values and another variable, say a_1, is:

$$r_{d_x a_1} = \frac{s_{x_2} r_{x_2 a_1} - s_{x_1} r_{x_1 a_1}}{\sqrt{s_{x_1}^2 + s_{x_2}^2 - 2 s_{x_1} s_{x_2} r_{x_1 x_2}}} \qquad [5]$$

If x_1, x_2, and a_1 are measured with no error, then $x_2 - x_1$ is true change, and $r_{d_x a_1}$ is without error. This, however, is a hypothetical situation rarely found in research. Kessler (1977) notes that difference scores are correlated with any error in component variables at both points in time. Furthermore, the difference score is composed of the positive value of x_2 and the negative value of x_1. Given the logic of a difference score, it is obvious that the difference score is related positively to the error in x_2 and negatively to the error in x_1 The result, not only is a spurious negative element in the correlation of a score at time 1 with the difference score (Bereiter, 1963), but also is a maximum parameter for difference-score reliability. A difference score's reliability can be no higher than the reliability of component scores (Kessler, 1977). Both Bohrnstedt (1969) and Kessler (1977) have shown that the difference score is highly unreliable.

A further problem with difference scores, discussed in detail by Kessler (1977), generally is referred to as "regression toward the mean." Both individual or single units of analysis at extreme ends of the variable's value range, and positive error components characteristic of extreme scores, tend to regress toward the mean when measured over time. This produces a deflating correlation and regression effect, respectively. Additionally, even if all variables are measured perfectly, a regression effect will occur. This is because of the spurious negative correlation between d_x and x_1, given the negative component of x_1 when the difference score is calculated. Because of these problems, Bohrnstedt (1969), Kessler (1977), and Cronbach and Furby (1970) recommend against the use of difference scores in correlational analyses.

One of the most common approaches to measuring change is proportions or percentages. A proportion, measuring relative change, is expressed as: x_2/x_1.

A value of 1.0 means that no change occurred. A value greater than 1.0 represents a relative increase from time 1; less than 1.0 reflects a relative decrease. Percentage change is simply an extension of the proportion:

$$\left(\frac{x_2}{x_1} - 1.0\right) * 100 \quad \text{or,} \quad \left(\frac{x_2 - x_1}{x_1}\right) * 100.$$

The logic of a proportion, percentage change, or difference score is that the amount of change should take into account the value of variable x at time 1. These three measures of change have been standards both in sociological and in demographic work.

Barclay (1958) and the U.S. Bureau of the Census (1975) suggest the use of proportions, percentages, or difference scores in the descriptive presentation of demographic data. In sociology, Loether and McTavish (1976) and Duncan et al. (1962) review these techniques as standard methods of presenting social data over time. Fuguitt and Thomas (1966) and Rogers et al. (1977) use percentage change in more sophisticated correlational computations.

Debate on the use of proportional and percentage change seems to center around two problems: (1) measures of relative change assume ratio level variables; few variables in sociology and not many more in demography are truly ratios; (2) the value of variable x at time 1 is not fully accounted for; this stems mainly from the unreliability and regression toward the mean arguments discussed for difference scores (Duncan et al., 1962; Kessler, 1977; Bohrnstedt, 1969).

A third approach to measuring change uses residualized difference scores. The goal of proportional and percentage change, and difference scores, is to construct a new variable to represent the concept of "change." Residualized difference scores "regress" out the influence of a variable's time 1 values from its time 2 values. The general form of the residualized difference score is (Bohrnstedt, 1969):

$$X_{2.1} = x_2 - \hat{x}_2 \qquad [6]$$

where

x_2 = observed score at time 2

$x_{2.1}$ = the residualized score for x_2 with the influence of x_1 "regressed out"

$\hat{x}_2$ = $b_0 + b_{x_2 x_1} x_1$. predicted x_2

b_0 = intercept constant

The intuitive appeal of this approach is threefold (Cronbach and Furby, 1970; Kessler, 1977): (1) by definition the covariance and correlation between $x_{2.1}$ and x_1 is zero; hence, the residual score is completely uncorrelated with the variable's initial score. An interpretation then deals with that part of the change in a variable that is unaccounted for by the variable's initial standing. (2) The regression problem is overcome: "it is unnecessary to enter [x_1] into a [future] regression equation, thus eluding the problem of confounded real cause with spurious regression effect" (Kessler, 1977: 55). (3) If the residual score is adjusted for unreliability, it gives an estimate of residual change that is more reliable than the simple difference score and does not have the statistical complexities of the difference score when adjusted for unreliability. However, the attractiveness of residualized difference scores diminishes because of two important problems. First, it cannot be determined how much of the observed difference over time is due to any given predictor because the effect due to x_1 is partialed out before change is calculated. Second, inasmuch as x_2 is regressed on x_1 before it is regressed on other independent variables, the correlation between x_1 and these other independent variables cannot be determined (Kessler, 1977: 55). Because of these two problems, residualized change scores are not recommended in correlational work (Bohrnstedt, 1969; Kessler, 1977).

The logic of residualized change scores, however, remains sound. When extended it leads to semipartial (i.e., part) and partial correlation (Bohrnstedt, 1969). If we continue to let a_1 represent time 1 values for variable a, and now define a_2 as a set of time 2 values for variable a, then the semipartial correlation between x_2 and a_1, with the influence of x_1 removed from x_2 but not a_1, is defined as:

$$r_{(x_2 \cdot x_1)a_1} = \frac{r_{x_2 a_1} - r_{x_1 a_2} r_{x_1 x_2}}{\sqrt{1.0 - r^2_{x_1 x_2}}} \qquad [7]$$

The partial correlation between x_2 and a_1, where x_1 is partialed out of both x_2 and a_1, is defined as:

$$r_{x_2 a_1 \cdot x_1} = \frac{r_{x_2 a_1} - r_{x_1 a_1} r_{x_1 x_2}}{\sqrt{1.0 - r^2_{x_1 a_1}} \sqrt{1.0 - r^2_{x_1 x_2}}} \qquad [8]$$

A decision must then be made as to which method of removing the influence of variable x at time 1 is most appropriate for studying the lagged correlation between x_2 and a_1.

Bohrnstedt (1969: 119) gives the following reason for choosing partial correlation over part correlation in the measurement of change:

> if x_1 and x_2 are positively correlated, as normally they will be, and x_1 and $[a_2]$ are positively correlated because of a causal relation, it is not unreasonable that the simultaneous correlation $[r_{x_2 a_2}]$ is positive. Therefore, when looking at the relationship of $[a_1]$ to x_2, one should partial the effect x_1 has on $[a_2]$ through $[a_1]$ since it is an artifact of the time-lagged causation that exists between $[a]$ and x. Or, stated differently, one should remove this indirect effect of x_1 on x_2 through $[a_1]$ by residualizing $[a_1]$ with x_1. When both x_2 and $[a_1]$ have been residualized by x_1 and then residuals are correlated, the result is simply $[r_{x_2 a_1 \cdot x_1}]$. Part correlation does not take into account the indirect effect that $[a_1]$ can have on x_2 through x_1 and, therefore, appears to be of little use in the study of causal change.

Partial correlation, therefore, seems to be the most appropriate measure where "cause" between two variables is time-lagged and there is need to remove the intervening effect of x_1 when the effect of a_1 on x_2 operates through x_1. Note that partial correlation skirts the issue of calculating a unique change variable but still allows a change interpretation. As demonstrated in the previous section, the logic of partial correlation extends to regression analysis in the multivariate case.

The relationship between the correlation coefficient and the regression coefficient in the bivariate case is simply:

$$r_{xa} = b_{xa} \left(\frac{s_a}{s_a} \right) \qquad [9]$$

When this is expanded into the change framework just discussed the relationship between the partial correlation and the three variable regression coefficient is defined as:

$$r_{x_2 a_1 \cdot x_1} = b_{x_2 a_1 \cdot x_1} \left(\frac{s_{a_1 \cdot x_1}}{s_{x_2 \cdot x_1}} \right) \qquad [10]$$

where

$s_{a_1 \cdot x_1}$ = standard error of estimate for a_1 and x_1 (i.e., the standard deviation of the residuals of a_1 regressed on x_1)

$s_{x_2 \cdot x_1}$ = standard error of estimate for x_2 and x_1 (i.e., the standard deviation of the residuals of x_2 regressed on x_1)

$b_{x_2 a_1 \cdot x_1}$ = regression coefficient of x_2 regressed on a_1 after x_1 (i.e., the partial covariance between the residual variables $x_2 \cdot x$ and $a_1 x_2$ divided by the partial variance—variance of the estimate—$s^2_{a_1 \cdot x_1}$)

The multivariate case with more than two variables at two points in time is simply an extension. For example, let c_1 represent values for c at time 1 and c_2 represent values for c at time 2. Expressed as a regression equation, the relationship between a_1 and x_2 controlling for x_1, c_1, and c_2 would be:

$$x_2 = b_o + b_{x_1} x_1 + b_{c_1} c_1 + b_{c_2} c_2 + b_{a_1} a_1 + e_{x_2} \quad [11]$$

where

b_o = intercept constant

$b_{x_1}, b_{c_1}, b_{c_2}, b_{a_1}$ = partial slope or regression coefficients

e_{x_2} = error.

At this point, it is appropriate to ask whether unstandardized or standardized coefficients (i.e., path coefficients derived from the regression analysis) would best serve the purposes of a multivariate longitudinal study. The correct answer is both! The relationship between the unstandardized regression coefficient and the standardized regression coefficient (beta) with two variables x and a is known to be:

$$B_{ax} = b_{ax} \left(\frac{s_x}{s_a} \right), \text{ when } b_{ax} \text{ is known or,} \quad [12]$$

$$b_{ax} = B_{ax} \left(\frac{s_a}{s_x} \right), \text{ when } B_{ax} \text{ is known} \quad [13]$$

Some authors recommend the use of standardized coefficients, some recommend unstandardized coefficients (see Blalock, 1971: 74, Blalock, 1964: 145-151). Standardized coefficients are most appropriate for intermodel comparisons, describing relationships in particular populations, or for interpreting the relative contribution of each variable. Unstandardized coefficients, however, are most appropriate for evaluating each variable in the model, stating general laws, or comparing populations. A major question decided by each researcher is whether the original unit of measurement is to be used when interpreting the model (i.e., unstandardized coefficients) or whether the originally measured units are to be transformed to a common scale before interpretation (i.e., standardized coefficients). However, standardized and unstandardized coefficients "correspond to different modes of interpretation that taken together give a deeper understanding of a situation than either can give by itself" (Wright, 1960: 202).

The use of a suitable longitudinal design is as important as the accurate measurement of change. It depends on the design of the research and appropriate assumptions. Path analysis is used in this article, although other approaches have been used in interpreting change and have been met with various degrees of acceptance. Foremost among these are the repeat measures analysis of variance (Huck and McLean, 1975; Lindquist, 1956), curve fitting and generating functions (Gottman et al., 1969; Cooley and Lohnes, 1971; Pendleton, 1976), cross-lagged correlations (Campbell, 1963; Holtzman, 1963; see also Ostrom, 1978), and for descriptive purposes, the complementary one group pretest-posttest design, and single and multiple time-series designs (Gottman et al., 1969; Campbell, 1963; Baltes, 1968; Lord, 1963). (These designs are not discussed here.)

PATH ANALYSIS AND
THE MEASUREMENT OF CHANGE

Path analysis has the ability to account for variable change over time. The logic of path analysis as change analysis is discussed by Blalock (1964), Duncan (1966), and Pelz and Andrews (1964), but not until Featherman's (1971a, 1971b) studies on socioeconomic achievement is the method clearly exposed.

Path analysis and causal inference refer to a procedure designed to bridge the gap between the theoretical and the empirical. It involves the construction of a structural equation model (Duncan, 1975), which leads to parameter estimation and evaluation for the support or refutation of a theory that links variables with notions of "x causes y" (Land, 1969). (Figures mapping paths between variables usually accompany the model of structural equations.) The ultimate goal of such a model

> is to define a set of equations which, in some sense, corresponds to actual causal processes in the real world; that is, one seeks a set of equations which permits predictions of how a *change* in any one variable in the system affects the values of other variables in the system [Heise, 1969: 41].

Although path analysis is somewhat controversial and has been called "faddish" both in demography and sociology, its correct application undeniably moves the construction and interpretation of theory two steps forward for every step backward.

The procedures of path analysis and causal inference operate within a set of necessary conditions. These assumptions are covered adequately by Heise (1969, 1970), Land (1969), Snedecor and Cochran (1973), Kerlinger and Pedhazur (1973), and Daniel (1974) and will not be repeated here. A very important characteristic of the causal assumptions covered by these authors is the time order of a system's variables, almost necessitating a longitudinal framework so as to accurately measure and test a path model.

Recognizing the difficulties of longitudinal methodologies and the measurement of change, Heise (1969: 43) offers the following explanation for an abundance of cross-sectional causal designs:

> the focus is on cause-effect changes that already have occurred— on measures [of] the changes after they have occurred rather than as they are occurring, and one presumes that at any one point in time some persons (groups, organizations) in the population have undergone a manipulation and others have not.

Still, longitudinal causal designs that account for the time order of systems variables are more desirable than cross-sectional designs (Land, 1969; Heise, 1969).

Featherman (1971a, 1971b) uses a logically simple but computationally complex prodedure for fitting the time order of variables into a path analytic framework. Others, including Land
and Felson (1976) and Featherman and Hauser (1976), incorporate the logic of Featherman's original approach, but modify it
in different directions. Very simply, any variable at time 1 is
entered into the model as an endogenous variable, avoiding
arguments of calculating a new change variable yet accounting
for the position of the variable at time 1 when evaluating the
position of the variable at time 2. Such a design also allows for the
identification of a spurious correlation or intervening effect
between another variable at time 1 (a_1) and the original variable
at time 2 (x_2) (as where x_1 serves as a confounding influence; this
was discussed earlier with the partial correlation example).

Featherman uses a complex longitudinal path model. A
variety of modifications that deviate from standard path analytic
research is required for clarity in the presentation of research
but its applicability seems sound. Its advantages over cross-
sectional models, however, have yet to be deliminated. For a
more clear understanding of such a model's composition, Figure 1
is presented with three variables both at time 1 and time 2.

Theoretically designated paths can be made in both the time
1 and time 2 planes. It must be assumed that each variable at time
1 can contribute to the "cause" of one or more variables at time 2
(both through direct and indirect paths). This requires the longitudinal designation of paths from each time 1 variable to *all*
time 2 variables unless there is sound theoretical reasoning for
this not to be so. Two major benefits of this approach not discussed previously are: (1) the design has a model-testing ability
which now assumes a longitudinal framework, and (2) the design
has a model-building approach, which allows for the empirical
designation of new, testable hypotheses derived from a theoretical framework.

However, this particular path model, as well as other longi-
tudinally designed path models, is susceptible to the problem of
correlated denominators. The problem of correlated denominators in path analysis as change analysis is discussed next.

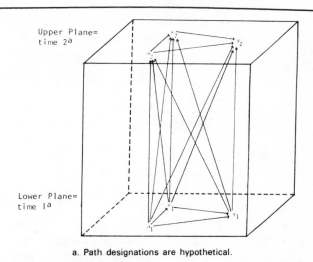

Upper Plane=
time 2[a]

Lower Plane=
time 1[a]

a. Path designations are hypothetical.

Figure 1: An Analytical Representation of the Longitudinal Path Model.

CORRELATED DENOMINATORS AND
CHANGE ANALYSIS IN PATH MODELS

The problem of correlated denominators in cross-sectional research was discussed in the first section of this article. The logic of the problem can now be briefly extended to the longitudinal design.

If d_2 is now variable d at time 2 and d_1 is variable d at time 1— both variables measured at each time period by the division of variable a by variable c (i.e., $d_2 = a_2/c_2$ and $d_1 = a_1/c_1$)—then their correlation is:

where

B_{ax} = standardized regression coefficient of a regressed on x (i.e., the regression coefficient expressed in standard score form)

b_{ax} = unstandardized regression coefficient of a regressed on x

s_x, s_a = standard deviations for x and a, respectively

$$r_{d_2 d_1} = \frac{r_{a_2 a_1} V_{a_2} V_{a_1} - r_{c_2 a_1} V_{c_2} V_{a_1} - r_{a_2 c_1} V_{a_2} V_{c_1} + r_{c_2 c_1} V_{c_2} V_{c_1}}{\sqrt{V_{a_2}^2 - 2r_{a_2 c_2} V_{a_2} V_{c_2} + V_{c_2}^2} \sqrt{V_{a_1}^2 - 2r_{a_1 c_1} V_{a_1} V_{c_1} + V_{c_1}^2}} \quad [14]$$

If $r_{a_2 a_1}$, $r_{a_2 c_2}$, $r_{c_2 a_1}$, and $r_{a_2 c_1}$ are all set to zero (i.e., if the intercorrelations of the rate's components are set to zero), the degree of spuriousness can be shown by:

$$r_{d_2 d_1} = \frac{r_{c_2 c_1} V_{c_2} V_{c_1}^2}{\sqrt{V_{a_2}^2 + V_{c_1}^2}\ \sqrt{V_{a_1}^2 + V_{c_1}^2}} \qquad [15]$$

When the correlations between denominators or rates at two points in time are high (e.g., $r_{c_2 c_1}$ is high), the spuriously inflated values may result in seriously misleading results. In the case of two rates, each measured at two points in time, the problem of correlated denominators and resulting spuriousness within the cross-sectional frame, in addition to the longitudinal frame, may result in seriously inflated values. It may be said that this is a variant of multicollinearity for the multivariate, longitudinal case in which variables are expressed as ratios. Although the expression of such a case (as in Figure 1) as a set of equations would be excessively complicated, we stress the point that the logic of the bivariate, longitudinal case (i.e., one variable measured at two points in time) is expandable to the multivariate longitudinal case (e.g., two variables measured at two points in time) as shown with bivariate and multivariate cross-sectional examples earlier. In the case of the path model presented as Figure 1, some problems of change analyses are overcome, but the problem of correlated denominators may remain.

As mentioned earlier, Freeman and Kronenfeld (1973) and our discussion on correlated denominators in cross-sectional analysis suggest the regression of a numerator on the denominator to remove or diminish the effect of correlated denominators. The resulting residual, while not directly interpretable, can then be used as a nonratio variable in correlational analyses. Most all longitudinal designs expressed with ratios will have denominators that are highly correlated, but not the same. Only in the rare longitudinal situation where the denominator is identical is it possible to redefine the relationship so that the common denominator is first entered into a regression equation as an additional independent variable (along with the numerators) for the purpose of partialling the influence of the common denominator. If this is attempted in the longitudinal design with ratios that have correlated but not identical denominators, the problem of multicollinearity (Blalock, 1963, 1964: 87-91) cannot be avoided. If, however, the longitudinal design is expressed with residuals, the correlation of these residuals will, within an expected margin of error, give results similar to those that would be obtained between ratios with small coefficients of variation for correlated denominators. Therefore, a multivariate longitudinal path model (like that in Figure 1), expressed as residuals at both points in time, will give values similar to those from a model expressed with rates that have small coefficients of variation for correlated denominators.

SUMMARY AND CONCLUSIONS

Ratio variables in sociological and demographic research often are calculated with denominators that are the same or highly correlated. This correlation between denominators (from high in magnitude to 1.0) may result in spurious statistical findings that are problematic in terms of conceptual and statistical interpretations and inferences. These errors may have repercussions when building or testing theory.

There were two general purposes of this article. One was to show, for sociologists and demographers, how the problem of correlated denominators expands from bivariate correlation and regression to partial correlation and multiple regression. The second purpose was to review advantages and disadvantages of three select techniques for measuring change: difference scores, proportions or percentages, and residualized difference scores. Then, path analysis as change analysis was focused on and the problem of correlated denominators in longitudinal path analysis was discussed. It can be suggested that, when all variables expressed as ratios in a model, including independent and dependent variables, have an identical denominator, or when the denominator of the dependent variable alone is to be held constant, the denominator may be entered into the standard least-squares regression framework as an independent variable. This, of course, serves to partial the problematic effect of identical denominators from relationships between numerators. However, in the case of correlated, yet not identical denominators, as is found in much cross-sectional research and almost invariably in longitudinal path analyses, this standard method of partialling cannot be used because the same effect (i.e., identical denominators) does not exist. Even if attempted, the problem of multicollinearity becomes inescapable. The use of residual analysis is suggested as one possible solution to the problem of correlated denominators both in cross-sectional and longitudinal research.

It is hoped that this article will further spur interest on correlated denominators in cross-sectional research, serve as a debut for the problem when applied to longitudinal research, and lead to further research investigating the use of residual and other statistical and conceptual analyses as solutions to the problem of correlated denominators.

NOTES

1. The distinction between a ratio and rate is ambiguous. The U.S. Bureau of the Census (1975: 8) notes that there is a tendency for "ratios" to be used for descriptive purposes; the sex ratio and dependency ratio are examples. "Rates" tend to be used in change analyses. The distinction, however, is difficult to define. This study uses the term ratio, which is meant to include "rate."

2. An excellent discussion of the various uses of ratio variables is presented by Bollen and Ward (1979). A major nonstatistical reason for ambiguity in the use of ratio variables rests with the conceptualization of the variable. The composition of a particular variable must reflect the intentions of a stated hypothesis (Gordon, 1968). Only when the hypothesis refers specifically to ratio variables is this difficulty overcome directly. Using, for example, income measured by per capita income and education measured by average education, even if this condition is met and per capita income is related to average education, the inference that person's income is causally dependent upon education drops one into the ecological fallacy (Robinson, 1950). Similarly, inferences made from per capita income or average education (referring to individual statuses) to income or education in general (referring to the aggregate) result in overgeneralizations (see also Blalock, 1964: 95-100; Bollen and Ward, 1979; Firebaugh, 1978; Burstein, 1978; Yule, 1910; and Pearson, 1910 for discussions related to these conditions).

REFERENCES

BAILEY, W. C., L. N. GRAY, and J. D. MARTIN (1971) "Communication." Social Problems 19: 284-289.
BALTES, P. B. (1968) "Longitudinal and cross sectional sequences in the study of age and generation effects." Human Development 11: 145-171.
BARCLAY, G. W. (1958) Techniques of Population Analysis. New York: John Wiley.
BEREITER, C. (1963) "Some persisting dilemmas in the measurement of change," pp.

3-20 in C. W. Harris (ed.) Problems in Measuring Change. Madison: Univ. of Wisconsin Press.

BLALOCK, H. M., Jr. (1971) "Four variable causal models and partial correlations," pp. 18-32 in H. M. Blalock, Jr. (ed.) Causal Models in the Social Sciences. Chicago: Aldine-Atherton.

——— (1964) Causal Inferences in Nonexperimental Research. Chapel Hill: Univ. of North Carolina Press.

——— (1963) "Correlated independent variables: the problem of multicollinearity." Social Forces 42: 233-236.

BOHRNSTEDT, G. W. (1969) "Observations on the measurement of change," pp. 113-116 in E. F. Borgatta and G. W. Bohrnstedt (eds.) Sociological Methodology: 1969. San Francisco: Jossey-Bass.

BOLLEN, K. and S. WARD (1979) "Ratio variables in aggregate data analysis: their uses, problems, and alternatives." Soc. Methods and Research 8 (May).

BURSTEIN, L. (1978) "Assessing differences between grouped and individual-level regression coefficients." Soc. Methods and Research 7: 5-28.

CAMPBELL, D. T. (1963) "From description to experimentation: interpreting trends as quasi experiments," pp. 212-244 in C. Harris (ed.) Problems in Measuring Change. Madison: Univ. of Wisconsin Press.

CHAYES, F. (1971) Ratio Correlation. Chicago: Univ. of Chicago Press.

CHIRICOS, T. G. and D. P. WALDO (1970) "Punishment and crime: an examination of some empirical evidence." Social Problems 18: 200-217.

COOLEY, W. W. and P. R. LOHNES (1971) Multivariate Data Analysis. New York: John Wiley.

CRONBACH, L. J. and L. FURBY (1970) "How should we measure 'change,' or should we?" Psych. Bull. 74: 68-80.

DANIEL, W. W. (1974) Biostatistics: A Foundation for the Health Sciences. New York: John Wiley.

DuBOIS, P. H. (1957) Multivariate Correlational Analysis. New York: Harper & Row.

DUNCAN, O. D. (1975) Introduction to Structural Equation Models. New York: Academic.

——— (1966) "Path analysis: sociological examples." Amer. J. of Sociology 72: 1-16.

——— R. P. CUZZORT, and B. DUNCAN (1962) Statistical Geography: Problems in Analyzing Areal Data. New York: Free Press.

FEATHERMAN, D. L. (1971a) "A research note: A social structural model for the socioeconomic career." Amer. J. of Sociology 77: 293-304.

——— (1971b) "Residential background and socioeconomic achievements in metropolitan stratification systems," Rural Sociology 36: 107-124.

——— and R. M. HAUSER (1976) "Changes in the socioeconomic stratification of the races, 1962-73." Amer. J. of Sociology 82: 621-651.

FIREBAUGH, G. (1978) "A rule for inferring individual-level relationships from aggregate data." Amer. Soc. Rev. 43: 557-572.

FLEISS, J. L. and J. M. TANUR (1971) "A note on the partial correlation coefficient." Amer. Statistician 25: 43-44.

FREEMAN, J. H. and J. E. KRONENFELD (1973) "Problems of definitional dependency: the case of administrative intensity." Social Forces 52: 108-121.

FUGUITT, G. V. and S. LIEBERSON (1974) "Correlation of ratios or difference scores having common terms," pp. 128-144 in H. L. Costner (ed.) Sociological Methodology 1973-1974. San Francisco: Jossey-Bass.

FUGUITT, G. V. and D. W. THOMAS (1966) "Small-town growth in the United States: an analysis by size, class and by place." Demography 3: 513-527.

GOLDFARB, N. (1960) Longitudinal Statistical Analysis. New York: Free Press.

GORDON, R. A. (1968) "Issues in multiple regression." Amer. J. of Sociology 73: 592-616.

GOTTMAN, J. M., R. M. McFALL, and J. T. BARNETT (1969) "Design and analysis of research using time series." Psych. Bull. 72: 299-306.

HARRIS, C. W. [ed.] (1963) Problems in Measuring Change. Madison: Univ. of Wisconsin Press.

HEISE, D. R. (1970) "Causal inference from panel data," pp. 3-27 in E. F. Borgatta and G. W. Bohrnstedt (eds.) Sociological Methodology: 1970. San Francisco: Jossey-Bass.

——— (1969) "Problems in path analysis and causal inference," pp. 38-73 in E. F. Borgatta and G. W. Bohrnstedt (eds.) Sociological Methodology: 1969. San Francisco: Jossey-Bass.

HOLTZMAN, W. H. (1963) "Statistical models for the study of change in the single case," pp. 199-211 in C. W. Harris (ed.) Problems in Measuring Change. Madison: Univ. of Wisconsin Press.

HUCK, S. W. and R. A. McLEAN (1975) "Using a repeated measures ANOVA to analyze the data from a pretest-posttest design: a potentially confusing task." Psych. Bull. 82: 511-518.

KERLINGER, F. N. (1973) Foundations of Behavioral Research. New York: Holt, Rinehart & Winston.

——— and E. L. PEDHAZUR (1973) Multiple Regression in Behavioral Research. New York: Holt, Rinehart & Winston.

KESSLER, R. C. (1977) "The use of change scores as criteria in longitudinal survey research." Quality and Quantity 11: 43-66.

KUH, E. and J. R. MEYER (1955) "Correlation and regression estimates when the data are ratios." Econometrica 23: 416-440.

LAND, K. C. (1969) "Principles of path analysis," pp. 3-37 in E. F. Borgatta and G. W. Bohrnstedt (eds.) Sociological Methodology: 1969. San Francisco: Jossey-Bass.

——— and M. FELSON (1976) "A general framework for building dynamic macro social indicator models: including an analysis of changes in crime rates and police expenditures." Amer. J. of Sociology 82: 565-604.

LINDQUIST, E. F. (1956) Design and Analysis of Experiments in Psychology and Education. Boston: Houghton Mifflin.

LOETHER, H. J. and D. G. McTAVISH (1976) Descriptive and Inferential Statistics. Boston: Allyn & Bacon.

LOGAN, C. H. (1972) "General deterrent effects of imprisonment." Social Forces 51: 64-73.

——— (1971) "On punishment of crime (Chiricos and Waldo, 1970): some methodology commentary." Social Problems 19: 280-284.

LORD, F. M. (1963) "Elementary models for measuring change," pp. 21-38, in C. W. Harris (ed.) Problems in Measuring Change. Madison: Univ. of Wisconsin Press.

MADANSKY, A. (1964) "Spurious correlation due to deflating variables." Econometrica 32: 652-655.

O'CONNOR, J. F. (1977) "A Logrithmic technique for decomposing change." Soc. Methods and Research 6: 91-102.

OSTROM, C. W. (1978) "Time series analysis: regression techniques." Sage University Paper Series on Quantitative Applications in the Social Sciences, 07-009. Beverly Hills: Sage.

PEARSON, K. (1910) "On the correlation of death rates." J. of the Royal Statistical Society 73: 534-539.

——— (1897) "Mathematical contributions to the theory of evolution: on a form of spurious correlation which may arise when indices are used in the measurement of organs." Proceedings of the Royal Society of London 60: 489-498.

PELZ, D. C. and F. M. ANDREWS (1964) "Detecting causal priorities in panel study data." Amer. Soc. Rev. 29: 836-848.

PENDLETON, B. F. (1977) Socioeconomic epidemiology: differential determinants in a longitudinal framework. Ph.D. dissertation, Department of Sociology, Iowa State University. (unpublished)

—— (1976) "A conceptual model for the identification, organization, and measure of influence of fertility policies and programs." Social Biology 23: 326-340.

PRZEWORSKI, A. and F. CORTES (1977) "Comparing partial and ratio regression models." Pol. Methodology 4: 63-75.

RANGARAJAN, C. and S. CHATTERJEE (1969) "A note on comparison between correlation coefficients of original and transformed variables." Amer. Statistician 23: 28-29.

ROBINSON, W. S. (1950) "Ecological correlations and the behavior of individuals." Amer. Soc. Rev. 15: 351-356.

ROGERS, D. L., B. F. PENDLETON, W. J. GOUDY, R. O. RICHARDS (1978) "Industrialization, income benefits, and the rural community." Rural Sociology 43: 250-264.

SCHUBNELL, H. and L. HERBERGER (1973) "The statistical problem of longitudinal analyses in demography." Proceedings of the 39th Session, Bulletin of the International Statistical Institute 45: 107-132.

SCHUESSLER, K. (1974) "Analysis of ratio variables: opportunities and pitfalls." Amer. J. of Sociology 80: 379-396.

—— (1973) "Ratio variables and path models," pp. 201-228 in A. S. Goldberger and O. D. Duncan (eds.) Structural Equation Models in the Social Sciences. New York: Seminar.

SNEDECOR, G. W. and W. G. COCHRAN (1973) Statistical Methods. Ames: Iowa State Univ. Press.

Social Science Research Council (1977) "Items." Social Science Research Council 31: 15.

—— (1976) "Items." Social Science Research Council 30: 48-49.

TITTLE, C. R. (1969) "Crime rates and legal sanctions." Social Problems 16: 409-423.

U.S. Bureau of the Census (1975) "The methods and materials of demography." H. S. Shryock, J. C. Siegel, and Associates (eds.) Washington, DC: Government Printing Office.

VANDERBOK, W. G. (1977) "On improving the analysis of ratio data." Pol. Methodology 4: 171-184.

WRIGHT, S. (1960) "Path coefficients and path regressions: alternative or complimentary concepts?" Biometrics 16: 189-200.

YULE, G. U. (1910) "On the interpretation of correlation between indices or ratios." J. of the Royal Statistical Society 73: 644-647.

Brian F. Pendleton is Assistant Professor of Sociology at the University of Akron. He is continuing research on ratio correlation and various demographic interests, concentrating on patterns of fertility and mortality.

Richard D. Warren is Professor of Sociology and Statistics at Iowa State University where he currently is pursuing research on organizational effectiveness and social indicators.

H. C. Chang is Associate Professor of Sociology at Iowa State University where he is pursuing research on migration and fertility. He recently returned from a sabbatical at National Taiwan University where he was engaged in fertility research.

THE GENERAL LINEAR MODEL
AND DIRECT STANDARDIZATION
A Comparison

6

RODERICK J.A. LITTLE
World Fertility Survey
THOMAS W. PULLUM
University of Washington

the purpose of this article is to sharpen the distinction and to clarify the relationship between two alternative ways of analyzing a common data structure. The structure to be assumed is an array of rates, means, or proportions, cross-classified in a nonorthogonal design with two or more predictor or control variables. The frequencies or case bases in each cell are known, but the researcher may not have access to the within-cell sums of squares. (Of course, the sums of squares are calculable if the cell entries are proportions.)

AUTHORS' NOTE: *The authors are listed in alphabetical order.*

The need to analyze such a structure is common, particularly in secondary analysis. For example, each Country Report issued through the World Fertility Survey (WFS) contains dozens of many-way tabulations of such a type, in which the cell entry is the mean number of children ever born, or the proportion wanting no more children, or the proportion using contraception, and so forth.

At one extreme of sophistication is some variant of direct standardization, such as the technique designated as Test Factor Standardization by Rosenberg (1962). Standardization has been used by demographers for decades and involves only simple calculations on a hand calculator. It is still occasionally used when more rigorous methods are accessible, as by Lieberson (1978) and by Clifford and Tobin (1977), but its use is easiest to justify when other methods are not available, as in many developing countries (Pullum, 1978).

At the other extreme, when computing facilities are at their best, many researchers would be inclined to use some variant of the General Linear Model (GLM) such as Multiple Classification Analysis. A discussion of these methods, some of which is repeated here, is given by Little (1978).

Our objective here is to reconsider the conditions under which standardization may be appropriate or inappropriate, and to reconsider the interpretation of its results, within the terminology of the general linear model. In no sense are we advocating increased use of standardization at the expense of more powerful models, but we seek to establish a formal linkage and to facilitate the correct use of a simple procedure.

In describing these approaches and in relating them we shall work with two main examples from the Fiji Fertility Survey, conducted in 1974. Table 2 gives the mean number of children ever born within categories of marital duration and education. This table is limited to Indian women, because there are pervasive ethnic differences in Fiji. Table 11 gives the proportion of Indian women who have ever used any efficient contraceptive method, within categories of current age, desire for more children, and education. For more details the reader may refer to the published report (Fiji, 1976) or to other WFS documentation.

STANDARDIZATION OF POPULATION QUANTITIES:
IMPLICATIONS

Let us consider a two-way cross-classification of means. Denote the variables as A and B with category labels i running from 1 to I and j running from 1 to J, respectively. In this section we shall assume that population data are available, so that no sampling is involved. Let μ_{ij} be the mean, rate, or proportion in row i and column j, and let ν_{ij} be the population base frequency in that cell. Let $\nu_{j\cdot}$ be the marginal frequency for row i, and μ_i the mean for row i, using the usual dot notation. Thus

$$\mu_{i\cdot} = \sum_j \mu_{ij}(\nu_{ij}/\nu_{i\cdot}) \quad (\text{where } \nu_{i\cdot} = \sum_j \nu_{ij}) \tag{1}$$

with weights $\nu_{ij}/\nu_{i\cdot}$ which sum to unity over j for all values of i.

Direct standardization with respect to variable B involves calculating row means with a new choice of weights $[\omega_j]$ which are the same for all values of i. Thus, the standardized mean for row i becomes

$$\mu_{i\cdot}(\omega) = \sum_j \mu_{ij}\omega_j. \tag{2}$$

with $\sum_j \omega_j = 1$. The set of weights $[\omega_j]$ is called the standard distribution and $\mu_{i\cdot}(\omega)$ represents the hypothetical mean that row i would have if B had this same distribution within each row.

A common choice of standard distribution is

$$\omega_j = \nu_{\cdot j} / \nu_{\cdot\cdot}, \tag{3}$$

which is the marginal distribution of B in the population. This is the form called Test Factor Standardization (TFS) and leads to standardized means

$$\mu_{i\cdot}^s = \sum_j \mu_{ij}(\nu_{\cdot j}/\nu_{\cdot\cdot}). \tag{4}$$

Another common choice of weights is $\omega_j = 1/J$ for all j, which leads to the unweighted row means.

As noted, the interpretation of the standardized means depends on the choice of standard distribution. However, often the analyst is more concerned with differences in the standardized means

$$\mu_{i.}(\omega) - \mu_{i'.}(\omega) = \Delta_{i,i'}(\omega) \quad \text{for } i \neq i' \qquad [5]$$

which represents the differences between levels of A when B has the same distribution $[\omega_j]$ within each level. Several authors, for example Kalton (1968) and Atchley (1969), have pointed out that the interpretation of these differences as the effects of A controlling B (or net of B) may be misleading when the differences are sensitive to the choice of standard distribution.

The artificial data in Table 1 (taken from Pullum, 1978) illustrate this phenomenon. In this table, when the effect of education on mean parity is controlled for marital duration using Test Factor Standardization, the difference between the low and high education groups is $(250 \cdot 4 + 250 \cdot 2)/500 - (250 \cdot 6 + 250 \cdot 2)/500 = -1.0$. That is, under this choice of standard distribution, higher-educated women would be said to have one child less than lesser educated women, controlling for marital duration. However, Table 1 shows that *within* levels of marital duration, the education effect is either 0.0 children (for low marital duration) or -2.0 (for high marital duration). Therefore the results of direct standardization will range from an education effect anywhere between 0.0 and -2.0, depending on choice of standard, is a misleading substitute for detailed examination of the table's interior.

Hence it is relevant to ask under what conditions the differences are the same for all choices of standard, that is,

$$\Delta_{i,i'}(\omega) = \Delta_{i,i'} \text{ for all } [\omega_j]. \qquad [6]$$

This condition is met if and only if the effects A and B are *linear additive,* according to the following definitions.

TABLE 1
**Mean Parity of Women Having Specified Levels of Education
and Marital Duration (hypothetical data)**

		Education	
		Low	High
Marital Duration	Low	2.0 (50)	2.0 (200)
	High	6.0 (200)	4.0 (50)

NOTE: Base Frequencies in Parentheses.

Definition 1. The effects of A and B are linear additive if and only if one of the following conditions holds: (a) differences in the row means are the same for all columns j, that is,

$$\mu_{ij} - \mu_{i'j} = \Delta_{i,i'} \text{ for all } j; \qquad [7]$$

(b) differences in the column means are the same for all rows i, that is,

$$\mu_{ij} - \mu_{ij'} = \Delta'_{j,j'} \text{ for all } i; \qquad [8]$$

(c) there exist constants $[\mu, \alpha_i, i = 1 \text{ to } I, \beta_j, j = 1 \text{ to } J]$ such that

$$\mu_{ij} = \mu + \alpha_i + \beta_j \text{ for all } i \text{ and } j. \qquad [9]$$

The equivalence of equations 7, 8, and 9 is well known and easily demonstrated. To show that equation 7 implies equation 6, note that if equation 7 holds then

$$\Delta_{i,i'}(\omega) = \sum_j \omega_j \mu_{ij} - \sum_j \omega_j \mu_{i'j} = \sum_j \omega_j \Delta_{i,i'} = \Delta_{i,i'} \text{ for all } [\omega_j].$$

To show that equation 6 implies equation 7, assume equation 6 and apply the particular set of weights $\omega_j = 1$, $\omega_j' = 0$ for $j \neq j'$ for each value of j in turn. We have thus established that equation 6 is equivalent to linear additivity. That is, differences in the standardized means can be intepreted unambiguously as effects of A net of, or controlling B if and only if A and B are linear additive. By contrast, if interaction terms γ_{ij} must be incorporated into equation 9, i.e., if A and B are not linear additive, then differences in standardized means will depend upon the magnitude of the interaction effects and the choice of weights. Such was the case for the hypothetical data in Table 1 discussed earlier.

There is one other situation where standardization can be used to calculate unambiguously the effects of A controlling B. Suppose that instead of calculating differences between the standardized means we calculate *ratios* of the standardized means $\delta_{i,i}'(\omega)$ = $\mu_i.(\omega) / \mu_{i'}(\omega)$, say. Alternative expressions of this quantity are $100 [\delta_{i,i}'(\omega) -1]$, the percentage difference between row i and row i', or $\log \delta_{i,i}'(\omega)$, which is the difference in the logarithm of the standaridized means of row i and row i', since $\log \delta_{i,i}'(\omega)$ = $\log \mu_{i.}(\omega) - \log \mu_{i'.}(\omega) = \Delta_{i,i}'(\omega)$, say.

These quantities are useful representations of the net effect of A if they are constant for all choices of weights, $[\omega_j]$. This condition of invariance is met if and only if the effects of A and B are *multiplicative, or log-linear additive*, according to the following definition.

Definition 2. The effects of A and B are log-linear additive (or multiplicative), if and only if one of the following conditions holds: (a) differences in the logarithms of the row means are the same for all columns; that is,

$$\log \mu_{ij} - \log \mu_{i'j} = \Delta_{i,i}' \text{ for all j;} \qquad [10]$$

(b) differences in the logarithms of the column means are the same for all rows i; that is,

$$\log \mu_{ij} - \log \mu_{ij'} = \Delta'_{j,j}' \text{ for all i;} \qquad [11]$$

(c) there exist constants $[\mu, \alpha_i, i = 1 \text{ to } I, \beta_j, j = 1 \text{ to } J]$ such that

$$\log \mu_{ij} = \mu + \alpha_i + \beta_j \text{ for all i and j.} \qquad [12]$$

It is easily shown, by analogy with the additive case, that log-linear additivity is equivalent to the invariance condition:

$$\log \mu_i. (\omega) - \log \mu_i'. (\omega) = \Delta_{i,i}' \text{ for all } [\omega_j]. \qquad [13]$$

The base of the logarithms in this definition is arbitrary. Equations 10 to 13 can be exponentiated to form a multiplicative analog to equation 9 and to show that if the effects of A and B are log-linear additive, the *ratios* between the standardized means of A are the same for all choices of standard and can be used to describe the effect of A controlling B.

SAMPLE ESTIMATION

So far we have considered only the structure of the population means of variables. We now apply these ideas to means from a sample of the population.

STANDARDIZATION OF SAMPLE MEANS

Suppose that we have a sample of size n_{ij} for the cell in row i, and column j, and an observed rate, mean, or proportion m_{ij} in that cell. The standardized mean for row i and standard distribution $[\omega_j]$ is

$$m_i. (\omega) = \sum_j m_{ij} \omega_j. \qquad [14]$$

Test Factor Standardization corresponds to the choice of weights

$$\omega_j = n_j / n.. \cdot$$

The following results are relevant: (a) suppose m_{ij} is an unbiased estimate of μ_{ij}. Then the expected values of the differences in the standardized sample means of A (or B) are the same for all choices of standard distribution if and only if A and B are linear additive. (b) Suppose that m_{ij} is an unbiased estimate of μ_{ij}. Then the expected values of the ratios of the standardized sample means of A (or B) are approximately the same for all choices of standard distribution if and only if A and B are log-linear additive. The approximation involves replacing the expected value of ratios by the ratio of expected values.

The implications of (a) are as follows: for any cross-classification, the differences of the standardized means $m_{i.}(\omega) - m_{i.}'(\omega)$ will vary according to the choice of standard, ω. However, if A and B are linear additive, these differences are always unbiased estimates of the population difference, which represents the effect of A controlling B. The choice of standard affects the sampling variance of the estimate, and the results of applying different standards differ only because of sampling fluctuation. On the other hand, if A and B are not linear additive, the differences of standardized means estimate different quantities for each choice of weights. A similar interpretation of (b) is obtained by replacing differences by log differences or ratios in this statement.

Example 1. The data in Table 2, taken from the 1974 Fiji Fertility Survey, consist of a cross-classification of the Mean Number of Children Ever Born (or Mean Parity) by two factors: A = Education, with four levels (1 = No Education, 2 = Lower Primary, 3 = Upper Primary, 4 = Secondary or Higher), and B = Years Since First Marriage (or Marital Duration), with six levels (1 = 0-4 years, 2 = 5-9 years, 3 = 10-14 years, 4 = 15-19 years, 5 = 20-24 years, 6 = 25 or more years). The first entry in each cell is the mean parity m_{ij} and the second entry is the sample size n_{ij}.

Primary interest in the table concerns the relationship between education and fertility. It appears that much of the large differences in the raw mean parities between educational levels is attributable to the compositional effect of marital duration, that is, to the fact that better educated women tend to be younger and to marry later than less educated women. It is of interest to estimate the relationship between education and fertility after con-

TABLE 2
Mean Number of Children Ever Born Since First Marriage
(for ever-married women of Indian race)

| | | Years Since First Marriage | | | (B) | | |
		0-4	5-9	10-14	15-19	20-24	25+	Mean
Educational								
Level (A)	1	.95 a)	2.80	4.14	4.93	6.20	7.18	5.19
		82 b)	93	118	151	160	288	892
	2	.97	2.69	3.90	5.43	6.03	7.49	4.21
		150	184	202	159	111	131	937
	3	.97	2.46	3.64	4.25	5.08	6.42	2.80
		188	149	99	63	48	31	578
	4	.72	2.08	2.89	3.20	3.40	2.00	1.53
		149	64	36	10	10	1	270
	Mean	.90	2.56	3.83	4.98	5.89	7.21	3.96
		569	490	455	383	329	451	2677

SOURCE: Fiji Fertility Survey, 1974.
a. First entry is mean number of children ever born.
b. Second entry is sample size.

trolling for marital duration. Hence we calculate means for each educational level standardized with respect to Marital Duration. We shall employ three standard distributions: (1) the marginal distribution of Marital Duration which corresponds to Test Factor Standardization; (2) the distribution giving the same weight to each level j of Marital Duration, which we call Equal Weights Standardization; and (3) the observed distribution of Marital Duration for the Secondary and Higher Educated women.

The weights for these distributions are given in Table 3 (rounded to two decimal places), and the standardized mean parities are given in Table 4. The last column of Table 4 gives the overall mean of the standardized education means, weighted by the total sample sizes in each education level. The low values for the third choice of standard reflects the prevalence of women with low marital durations and hence low parities among women with Secondary and Higher Education. When these means are sub-

TABLE 3
Weights for the Three Standard Distributions of Marital Duration (to be applied to Table 2)

	Marital Duration Category						
Standard	1	2	3	4	5	6	Total
1) Test factor	.21	.18	.17	.14	.12	.17	1.00
2) Equal Weights	.17	.17	.17	.17	.17	.17	1.00
3) Secondary and Higher	.55	.24	.13	.04	.04	.00	1.00

tracted from the standardized parities in the same row, we obtain the deviations given in parentheses. Result (a) implies that the deviations in Table 4 will have the same expectation for all standards if the effects of A and B are linear additive. However, we note that in this example these deviations appear to be sensitive to the choice of standard: for example, the women with secondary and higher education have 1.58 children less than the mean after TFS, but only .53 less than the mean after standardization with the marital duration distribution of the Secondary and Higher Education group.

Although no statistical test has been applied, this seems to suggest that the effects of A and B are not linear additive. In fact linear additivity can be discredited from theoretical considerations. The assumption implies that differentials in mean parity between education groups are the same for all levels of marital duration and this is clearly not appropriate; in the absence of premarital births, the mean parity of each group at marriage duration zero is zero, and hence differences are also zero. Differences between education groups emerge only as marital duration increases, and hence the effects of education and marital duration cannot be additive.

In contrast, the assumption that the effects are log linear additive, that is, *percentage* differences in mean parity between education groups are the same for all marriage durations, seems much more plausible as a working hypothesis. Accordingly we present

TABLE 4
Standardized Mean Parities (as a result of the application
to Table 2 of the three standard distributions of
marital duration)

	Educational Level				Overall Mean (Weighted)
Standard	1	2	3	4	
1) Test Factor	4.10	4.14	3.59	2.24	3.82
	(.28)	(.32)	(-.23)	(-1.58)	
2) Equal Weights	4.37	4.42	3.80	2.38	4.06
	(.31)	(.36)	(-.26)	(-1.68)	
3) Secondary and Higher	2.18	2.15	1.97	1.53	2.06
	(-.12)	(-.09)	(-.09)	(-.53)	

Deviations from the overall mean under each standard are given in parentheses.

the effects of education as percentage deviations of the standardized means from the overall standardized mean, with the results given in Table 5. It is clear that the percentage deviations are less sensitive to the choice of standard, thus lending support to this method of presentation and to the assumption of underlying log-linear additivity.

RELATIONSHIP TO MULTIPLE CLASSIFICATION ANALYSIS

We have noted that standardization has a particularly simple interpretation when the effects of A and B are linear additive. Thus in situations where this is plausible it makes sense to consider alternative estimates of the cell means μ_{ij} which exploit this additivity assumption. Recall that if A and B are linear additive then the population means can be written as $\mu_{ij} = \mu + \alpha_i + \beta_j$ for all i and j, for suitable choices of μ, α_i, and β_j. Hence we calculate estimates $\hat{\mu}$, $\hat{\alpha}_i$, and $\hat{\beta}_j$ from the data and replace the sample means by fitted values

$$\hat{\mu}_{ij} = \hat{\mu} + \hat{\alpha}_i + \hat{\beta}_j \text{ for all i and j.} \qquad [15]$$

The constants $\hat{\mu}$, $\hat{\alpha}_i$, and $\hat{\beta}_j$ are chosen so that the fitted values are as close as possible to the sample means. More precisely, they

TABLE 5
Standardized Mean Parities (when the standard distributions in Table 3 are applied to the logarithms of the parities in Table 2)

Standard	Educational Level				Overall Mean (Weighted)
	1	2	3	4	
1) Test Factor	4.10 (7.4)	4.15 (8.6)	3.59 (-5.9)	2.24 (-41.3)	3.82
2) Equal Weights	4.36 (7.5)	4.41 (8.7)	3.80 (-6.4)	2.38 (-41.4)	4.06
3) Secondary and Higher	2.18 (5.9)	2.15 (4.3)	1.98 (-4.1)	1.53 (-25.7)	2.06

NOTE: Percentage deviations from the overall means under each standard are given in parentheses.

are chosen so that the weighted sum of squares

$$S S = \sum_{i,j} n_{ij} (\hat{\mu}_{ij} - m_{ij})^2 \qquad [16]$$

is minimized. This procedure is the special case of additive analysis of variance called multiple classification analysis (MCA). It is optimal when the within cell variance is constant (of course, it will not be constant when the cell entry is a proportion, a case to be discussed below); a more general form is to minimize

$$\sum_{i,j} k_{ij} n_{ij} (\hat{\mu}_{ij} - m_{ij})^2$$

for some choice of constants k_{ij}.

This estimation of the cell means entails some extra computation. However, fitted values have certain advantages for the sample means, m_{ij}. (a) The fitted means can be calculated for cells with no observations; (b) the fitting process smooths the estimates for cells with small sample sizes, thus reducing the effect of sampling variance; (c) when within-cell sums of squares are known, the linear additivity assumption can be tested by an analysis of variance F-test, which essentially compares the minimized value of equation 16 with the average within-cell variance. Also, the statistical significance of the effects of A controlling B can be calculated.

Having obtained estimates of the cell means in this way, we can present the effects of A controlling B by standardizing the fitted values from equation 15. Then the standardized fitted values $\hat{\mu}_{i.}(\omega) = \sum_j \hat{\mu}_{ij}\omega_j$ clearly depend on the choice of standard distribution. However, the *differences* in the standardized fitted means are the same for any choice of standard, for

$$\hat{\mu}_{i.}(\omega) - \hat{\mu}_{i'.}(\omega) = \sum_j (\hat{\mu}_{ij} - \hat{\mu}_{i'j})\,\omega_j$$

$$= \sum_j (\hat{\alpha}_i - \hat{\alpha}_{i'})\,\omega_j = \hat{\alpha}_i - \hat{\alpha}_{i'} \quad \text{for all } \{\omega_j\}. \qquad [17]$$

Hence these estimates of the effects of A net of B are the same for any choice of standard, an attractive property not shared by estimates from the observed means.

Example 2. Consider again the data in Table 2 discussed in the previous section. Multiple classification analysis is *not* appropriate for this table since there are strong theoretical reasons for rejecting the assumption of linear additivity of effects. Despite this we shall apply it here for illustrative purposes. The fitted values are given in Table 6. The additive structure of the fitted values can be readily verified; for example, the difference between the first two rows is .03 for all columns (apart from some rounding). Using these fitted values, we obtain estimates of mean parity within educational levels, standardized by marital duration, as given in Table 7.

It is clear that the differences between the educational categories are the same for all choices of standard, as required by equation 17. Equivalently, the difference between each category and the overall (standardized) mean is the same for every choice of standard: .16, .19, −.27, and −.61 for educational levels 1, 2, 3, and 4, respectively.

RELATIONSHIP WITH LOG-LINEAR MODELS

We have noted that there are situations (such as the example above) when a linear additive model, with the consequent estima-

TABLE 6
Fitted Mean Parities for Table 2
(using MCA and the implausible assumption of
linear additivity)

		Years Since First Marriage					
		0–4	5–9	10–14	15–19	20–24	25+
Educational Level	1	1.24	2.79	3.97	5.06	5.97	7.23
	2	1.27	2.81	4.00	5.09	6.00	7.26
	3	.81	2.35	3.53	4.63	5.54	6.79
	4	.46	2.00	3.19	4.28	5.19	6.45

tion of net effects as differences of standardized means, is not realistic but a log-linear additive model, with the consequent estimation of net effects as the ratios of standardized means, is appropriate. Under these circumstances it is natural to replace the cell means $m_{.j}$ by estimates of μ_{ij} which take the form

$$\log\hat{\mu}_{ij} = \hat{\mu} + \hat{\alpha}_i + \hat{\beta}_j \text{ for all i and j} \qquad [18]$$

where $\hat{\mu}$, $\hat{\alpha}_i$, $\hat{\beta}_j$ are chosen so that the $\hat{\mu}_{ij}$ are in some sense close to the sample means. The usual criterion is to minimize the chi-squared statistic

$$X^2 = \sum_{i,j} n_{ij} m_{ij} \log(\hat{\mu}_{ij}/m_{ij}). \qquad [19]$$

This is a variant of the generalized linear model, as discussed by Nelder and Wedderburn (1972). Note that despite formal similarities, the model equation 18 is conceptually distinct from the log-linear models for contingency tables developed by Goodman (1972), since here we are dealing with a cross-classification of means and not a two-way table of counts. Contingency tables will be discussed below.

As before, we can standardize these fitted values, forming $\hat{\mu}_{i.}(\omega) = \sum_j \hat{\mu}_{ij}\omega_j$. It is now clear that *ratios* of these quantities or differences in their logarithms are the same for all choices of

TABLE 7
Standardized Mean Parities: Three Standard
Distributions in Table 3 Applied to the Fitted
Data in Table 6

	Educational Level				Overall Mean
Standard	1	2	3	4	
1) Test Factor	4.12	4.15	3.69	3.35	3.96
2) Equal Weights	4.38	4.41	3.94	3.60	
3) Secondary and Higher	2.31	2.34	1.88	1.54	2.15

standard distribution. This follows from the equivalence of equations 12 and 13 applied to the fitted values $\hat{\mu}_{ij}$. Specifically,

$$\log \hat{\mu}_{i.}(\omega) - \log \hat{\mu}_{i'.}(\omega) = \hat{\alpha}_i - \hat{\alpha}_{i'} \text{ for all } [\omega_j],$$

so that the differences in the log standardized means are simply differences in the row parameters in equation 18.

If the effects are believed to be log-linear additive, the analyst is faced with a choice of presenting ratios of standardized means with or without smoothing by fitting the appropriate model. Fitting the model requires more work, but provides estimates for any empty cells, is statistically efficient and allows the assumption of log-linear additivity to be tested, for example by a chi-squared test on the minimized value of X^2.

Example 3. An additive log-linear model was fitted to the data in Table 2, using the computer package GLIM (General Linear Interactive Modeling). For those familiar with GLIM, this is achieved by specifying a Poisson error structure and a weight variable equal to the sample size in each cell. The fitted values are given in Table 8; the multiplicative structure can be verified by checking that ratios between rows are the same for all columns. (It is also worth noting that these fitted values are closer to the observed means in Table 2 than those obtained from the additive model in Table 6. This reflects the superiority of the log-linear

TABLE 8
Fitted Mean Parities for Table 2
(using the assumption of log-linear additivity)

		Years Since First Marriage					
		0-4	5-9	10-14	15-19	20-24	25+
Educational Level	1	1.02	2.75	4.00	5.09	6.03	7.24
	2	1.03	2.79	4.05	5.15	6.10	7.33
	3	.90	2.43	3.54	4.50	5.33	6.40
	4	.71	1.92	2.79	3.56	4.21	5.06

model for these data.) Using these fitted values, we obtain the estimates of mean parity within educational levels, standardized by marital duration, given in Table 9. It is readily verified that the percentage deviations of the standardized means from the overall mean are the same for all these standardizations: 5.6%, 6.8%, −6.8%, and −26.4% for educational levels 1, 2, 3, and 4, respectively. These estimates can be compared with the percent deviations derived from the observed table given above. The results from the Secondary and Higher standard are closest to those from the log-linear model, partly because the other standards appear to lead to an underestimate of the fertility of the secondary and higher educated group. The underestimate is caused by the low observed means for this group in the 20-24 and 25+ categories of Marital Duration, and the relatively high weights given to these cells in Test Factor and Equal Weights Standardization. One effect of fitting the model is to revise upwards the estimated fertility of these cells, resulting in an increase in the estimated fertility for this group from 41% below the mean (see above) to 26% below the mean.

It should be noted that the model fitting process also provides statistical evidence on the fit of the model and the significance of the effects. The log-linear additive model yielded a chi-squared of 16.07 on 15 degrees of freedom, indicating that the model fits the data. A log-linear model assuming no effect of Education yielded a chi-squared of 82.16 on 18 degrees of freedom, highly significant, indicating that this model does not fit the data. The conclu-

TABLE 9
Standardized Mean Parities: Three Standard
Distributions in Table 3 Applied to the Fitted
Data in Table 8

Standard	Educational Level				Overall Mean
	1	2	3	4	
1) Test Factor	4.09	4.14	3.62	2.86	3.88
2) Equal Weights	4.36	4.41	3.85	3.04	4.13
3) Secondary and Higher	2.19	2.21	1.93	1.53	2.07

sions are that the effect of Education, controlling for Marital Duration, is statistically significant, and the effect of Marital Duration and Education can be considered additive on the log-linear scale. Confidence limits for the percentage differences in parity between education levels can also be derived.

MULTIWAY CROSS-CLASSIFICATIONS OF MEANS

The results thus far are easily generalized to tables of any dimension. To simplify the notation we shall consider only three-way tables of means; the extension to higher order tables will be clear from this case.

Consider a three-way cross classification of means. Denote the variables as A, B, and C with category labels i running from 1 to I, j running from 1 to J and k running from 1 to K. Let μ_{ijk} be the population mean in row i, column j and panel k, and let ν_{ijk} be the population base frequency for that cell.

Let

$$\left\{ \omega_{jk}, \ j = 1 \text{ to } J, \ k = 1 \text{ to } K, \ \sum_{j,k} \omega_{jk} = 1 \right\}$$

be a standard distribution over the factors B and C. Then the corresponding standardized mean for row i is

$$\mu_{i..}(\omega) = \sum_{j,k} \mu_{ijk} \omega_{ijk}.$$

Differences in the (log) standardized means between two rows are the same for all choices of standard distribution if and only if the effects of A and BC are (log) linear additive, where BC is the joint factor consisting of all pairs of levels of B and C. These comparisons (on the approprite scale) then represent the effect of A, controlling B and C.

Note that the joint control of B and C does not require that the effects of B and C are additive. In the notation of log-linear models, the condition is that the data fit the model [A, BC]. If the data fit the stronger model [A,B,C] which assumes the effects of A, B, and C are additive, then standardized means of B and C can also be interpreted as the net effects of those variables, since the model [A,B,C] implies the models [AC,B] and [AB,C].

CONTINGENCY TABLES

So far we have considered applications of standardization to cross-classification of means. In this section we consider contingency tables and in particular the relationship between standardization and the system of log-linear models for contingency tables given by Goodman (1970, 1972) and discussed in Davis (1974) or Bishop et al. (1975).

A contingency table presents the joint distribution of counts over a set of factors, whereas standardization concerns the relationship of one response variable to a set of other factors. Thus for our purposes it is necessary to define a response variable and to consider variation in the conditional distribution of that variable over the other variables. It will be sufficient to consider a dichotomous response variable. If there are more than two categories, say K, one can successively dichotomize each of K-1 categories against the remainder.

Accordingly consider the IxJx2 contingency table with three factors A, B, and C and category labels i running from 1 to I, j running from 1 to J and k taking the values 0 and 1, respectively. Let ν_{ijk} be the population count in row i, column j, and level k; that is, we assume that no sampling is involved. We are interested in the distribution of C within combinations of A and B. Accordingly, for each i and j we form the proportion with C = 1, referred to as π_{ij}, based on frequency $\nu_{ij.} = \nu_{ijo} + \nu_{ij1}$, so that

$$\pi_{ij} = \nu_{ij1}/\nu_{ij.}. \tag{20}$$

Then the conditional distribution of C given A and B can be studied using this two-way table of proportions.

Note that each proportion is also the mean of the variable C, and hence we have a table of means as discussed in previous sections, the only difference being that the response variable is dichotomous. Hence the results of the previous sections can be applied. That is, differences in the standardized proportions are appropriate if effects A and B are linear additive, and ratios are appropriate if the effects A and B are log linear additive.

However, neither of these conditions corresponds to a log linear model for the I X J X 2 contingency table. Consider the log linear model for the frequencies

$$\log \nu_{ijk} = \lambda + \lambda_i^A + \lambda_j^B + \lambda_k^C + \lambda_{ij}^{AB} + \lambda_{ik}^{AC} + \lambda_{jk}^{BC} \quad \text{for all i, j, k,} \tag{21}$$

which is the model which fixes the AB, AC, and BC margins, and thus can be written [AB,AC,BC] in the notation of Goodman (1970). Note that equation 21 is the most general model short of the saturated model. The following comments apply to all log linear models for the frequencies which exclude three-way interactions between (a) the predictor, (b) the control, and (c) the dependent variable.

What model does equation 21 imply for the table of *proportions*? Note that from equations 20 and 21

$$\pi_{ij}/(1 - \pi_{ij}) = \nu_{ij1}/\nu_{ijo},$$

so

$$\log \left[\pi_{ij}/(1 - \pi_{ij}) \right] = \log \nu_{ij1} - \log \nu_{ijo}$$

$$= (\lambda_1^C - \lambda_0^C) + (\lambda_{i1}^{AC} - \lambda_{i0}^{AC}) + (\lambda_{j1}^{BC} - \lambda_{j0}^{BC}).$$

Hence $\log \left[\pi_{ij}/(1 - \pi_{ij}) \right] = \mu + \alpha_i + \beta_j$ \hfill [22] for suitable choices of μ, α_i, and β_j. Thus the log linear model equation 21 corresponds to an additive model for log $[\pi_{ij}/(1 - \pi_{ij})]$ in the table of proportions. This transformation of the proportions is the familiar logit or log-odds function: logit $\pi_{ij} = \log[\pi_{ij}/(1-\pi_{ij})]$, and accordingly, equation 22 is called a *logit linear additive model*, and variables A and B satisfying this model are called *additive on the logit scale*.

In general, log linear models for contingency tables imply logit linear models for proportions. The relationship is discussed in more detail in Goodman (1970). Aside from this theoretical link, there is a practical reason for considering the logit transformation for tables of proportions: if a logit-linear model is calculated then the fitted values always lie between zero and one.

If equation 21 holds, then equation 22 implies that differences between standardized logits will be invariant with respect to the choice of standard. That is, differences of the form

$$\sum_j (\text{logit } \pi_{ij}) \, \omega_j - (\text{logit } \pi_{i'j}) \, \omega_j \qquad [23]$$

will not depend upon the choice of $[\omega_j]$. However, above it was the means themselves that were standardized, and then differences between the standardized means or the logs of the standardized means were found to be invariant according to whether the underlying structure was linear additive or log linear additive. We are motivated to ask whether, in the present case, any transformation of the standardized means (i.e., proportions) has the invariance property. For this purpose we shall consider an example.

Example 4. Consider the artificial table of proportions in Table 10. The effects of A and B are logit linear additive, as can be seen from the corresponding logits in Table 10 (ii). The difference between A = 1 and A = 2 is 2.0 on the logit scale within all the categories of B (controlling for B). As a result, standardization of the logits will be invariant with respect to the choice of standard: differences of the form equation 23 do not depend on the choice of $[\omega_j]$ and always equal 2.0.

TABLE 10
Standardization of a Logit-Linear Additive
Table of Proportions

(i) Table of Proportions

		Factor B		
		1	2	3
Factor A	1	.119	.269	.500
	2	.018	.047	.119

(ii) Table of Logits

Factor A	1	-2.0	-1.0	0.0
	2	-4.0	-3.0	-2.0

(iii) Comparisons of Standardized Proportions Within Categories of A, using Various Standard Distributions of B

	Standard Distribution			Standardized Proportions		Differences in Standardized Proportions		
				Factor A		Raw	Log	Logit
				1	2			
a)	1	0	0	.119	.018	.101	1.889	2
b)	3/5	2/5	0	.179	.030	.149	1.786	1.953
c)	3/5	1/5	1/5	.225	.044	.181	1.632	1.842
d)	1/3	1/3	1/3	.296	.061	.235	1.574	1.868
e)	1/5	1/5	3/5	.378	.084	.293	1.504	1.891
f)	0	0	3/5	.408	.090	.317	1.508	1.937
g)	0	0	1	.500	.119	.381	1.436	2

The last three columns of Table 10 (iii) give, for seven arbitrary standard distributions labelled (a) to (g), the differences between three functions of the standardized proportions, namely

Raw: $\pi_1.(\omega) - \pi_2.(\omega)$,   [24]

Log: $\log \pi_1.(\omega) - \log \pi_2.(\omega)$,   [25]

Logit: $\text{logit } \pi_1.(\omega) - \text{logit } \pi_2.(\omega)$.   [26]

Note that all three sets of differences are sensitive to the choice of standard distribution. This example is sufficient to prove that none of these transformations has the invariance property, and it can be shown that, in fact, *no transformation of the standardized proportions* has the invariance property if A and B are logit linear additive.

Nevertheless, Table 10 (iii) shows that differences in the logits (equation 26) are least sensitive to the choice of standard, varying

TABLE 11
Portion of Indian Women in Fiji Who Ever Used an Efficient Contraceptive Method According to Current Age, Desire for More Children and Educational Level

Education	Desire For More Children		INDIANS Age			
			1	2	3	4
LOW	YES	p	.60	.72	.58	.42
		n	247	163	135	19
LOW	NO	p	.82	.89	.90	.84
		n	67	160	497	306
HIGH	YES	p	.65	.82	.69	.67
		n	281	131	54	3
HIGH	NO	p	.84	.88	.91	.81
		n	50	101	133	47

p = proportion

n = sample size

SOURCE: Fiji Fertility Survey, 1974

in this example from 2.0 to 1.868, compared with variations of .101 to .381 in the raw differences (equation 24) and 1.889 to 1.436 in the logs (equation 25).

We have seen that when a table of proportions has a logit-linear additive structure, the constant difference in the logits between rows cannot be recovered from the standardized raw proportions for all choices of standard distribution. The relationship between logit-linear models and standardization for tables of proportions is at best approximate, resting in the replacement of equation 23 by equation 26.

This appears to limit the usefulness of standardization for observed tables of proportions where the logit-linear additive structure is believed to apply. The estimated effects from fitting the correct logit-linear model cannot be approximated from standardized proportions and are lost by standardizing the table of fitted proportions. Nevertheless, in some cases this theoretical limitation can be ignored, for the following reasons. (a) For proportions lying between 0.2 and 0.8, the logit scale is approximately linear and thus log-linear additivity is nearly the same as linear additivity. Thus if most observed proportions in a table lie within this range, the analyst can safely consider raw differences in the standardized proportions. (b) For proportions of less than 0.2, the logit scale closely resembles the log scale. Thus if all the observed proportions are small, the analyst may consider percentage differences in the standardized proportions. Similarly, if all the observed proportions are close to one, the analyst may replace each proportion by unity minus the proportion and again consider percentage differences in the standardized proportions, with appropriate interpretation. (c) For cases not covered by (a) or (b), the best approximate procedure is probably to consider the standardized logits, although the interpretation of these as log-odds is not quite as familiar as the other forms. We conclude the discussion by applying these suggestions to our final example.

Example 5. The proportions in Table 11 are derived from a 2x4x2x2 contingency table which gives the number of women who have never used modern contraception, within two categories of education, four categories of age, and two categories of fertility preference (whether the woman does or does not want children). As with Table 2, the data refer to Indian women in the Fiji Fertility Survey, 1974. Ever-use by women who want more children will have been primarily for spacing purposes.

These data are reorganized in Table 12 such that preferences and age are combined into an 8-category variable, and the interest is in the effect of education upon ever-use controlling for preferences and age simultaneously. From the preceding discussion, standardization will be an acceptable method for controlling so long as the differences (equation 23) do not depend upon the choice of standard. To check this, we have applied two alternative standards: the uniform distribution, in which one-eighth of the sample is in each of the preference x age categories, and TFS, which uses the overall sample frequencies in the final column of Table 12.

Under the uniform distribution, the standardized logit is 1.382 for the higher educated group and 1.108 for the less educated

TABLE 12
Proportion (and Logit) of Indian Women in Figi Who Ever Used an Efficient Contraceptive Method According to Current Age, Desire for More Children, and Educational Level

Desire for Another Child	Age Group	High Education		Low Education		Sample Size
		Proportion	Logit	Proportion	Logit	
Yes	1	.65	.619	.60	.455	528
Yes	2	.82	1.516	.72	.944	294
Yes	3	.69	.800	.58	.323	189
Yes	4	.67	.709	.42	-.323	22
No	1	.84	1.658	.82	1.515	117
No	2	.88	1.992	.89	2.091	261
No	3	.91	2.314	.90	2.197	630
No	4	.81	1.450	.84	1.658	353

SOURCE: Table 11.
NOTE: Logits calculated from proportions before rounding.

group, for a difference in standardized logits of .274. Under Test Factor Standardization the quantities are 1.513 and 1.363, respectively, for a difference of .150. The differences (.274 and .150) depend heavily upon the choice of standard, and we conclude without making a formal test that standardization is not appropriate.

The application of logit linear models to the original 2x4x2x2 table shows that, as might have been expected from theoretical considerations, there is significant interaction between education and preferences. That is, education and the preference x age composite variable are not logit linear additive in their impact on ever-use, a formal confirmation that standardization is not appropriate.

Pursuing this illustration a bit further, we can focus on the women who state a desire for no more children, and consider (within this group) the effect of education controlling for age. There is only a small sensitivity to choice of standard in the difference between standardized logits. Under the uniform age distribution, the difference between the high and low education categories is –.012 on the logit scale; using the overall age distribution for these women, the difference is –.006. With the age distribution of the lower educated women as the standard, the difference is –.011, and with the age distribution of the higher educated women as the standard, the difference changes sign to .009. The variation is small. Calculation of the logit linear models for these data using ECTA (Everyman's Contingency Table Analysis) shows that (a) there is no significant education effect, controlling for age, and (b) the preceding four numbers are inside the 95% confidence interval for the education effect on the logit scale.

SUMMARY AND CONCLUSION

We have seen that standardization of a table of means is an efficient summarization of data if differences in the standardized means, on the raw or log scale, are insensitive to the choice of standard. This corresponds to certain linear or log-linear models for the table, which express that the effects of the factors on the response are additive, or in other words, that interactions are not present in the data. The first difficulty in using standardization is in deciding whether such significant interactions are present. Approximate tests of additivity could be developed but have not been given here. Even if this condition is met, there will be some statistical variation in the differences between (or ratios of) standardized quantities as different standards are used. This leads to a second difficulty, namely that standardization leads to statistically inefficient estimates of standardized differences and can be oversensitive to deviant cell means based on small numbers of observations.

An alternative procedure is to use the underlying additivity assumption to fit appropriate models to the data, such as the linear additive models of analysis of variance or log-linear additive models. Then the fitted means from these models can be standardized rather than observed means. The resulting standardized differences are completely insensitive to the choice of standard and are under certain assumptions statistically efficient. Also the fitting procedure can include formal statistical tests of the additivity assumption.

If a table of proportions is derived from a multidimensional contingency table, these can also be subjected to direct standardization. However, in such cases the condition of linear or log linear additivity is not the most natural; the conditions corresponding to log-linear models for the contingency table is that the table of proportions is additive on the logit scale. If logit-linear additivity applies, then no transformation of differences in the standardized proportions is entirely appropriate, although raw differences, or log differences, are approximately valid in certain situations, and in such cases can serve as approximations to the estimated effects from the logit-linear additive model.

REFERENCES

ATCHLEY, R. (1969) "A qualification of test factor standardization." Social Forces 47: 84-85.
BISHOP, Y.M.M., S. E. FIENBERG, and P. W. HOLLAND (1975) Discrete Multivariate Analysis. New York: John Wiley.
CLIFFORD, W. B. and P. L. TOBIN (1977) "Labor force participation of working mothers and family formation: some further evidence." Demography 14: 273-284.
DAVIS, J. A. (1974) "Hierarchical models for significance tests in multivariate contingency tables: an exegesis of Goodman's recent papers," in H. L. Costner (ed.) Sociological Methodology, 1973-1974. San Francisco: Jossey-Bass.
Fiji (1976) The Fiji Fertility Survey 1974—Principal Report. Suva, Fiji: Printing and Stationery Department.
GOODMAN, L. A. (1972) "A general model for the analysis of surveys." Amer. J. of Sociology 77: 1035-1086.
——— (1970) "The multivariate analysis of qualitative data: interactions among multiple classifications." J. of the Amer. Statistical Association 65: 225-256.
KALTON, G. (1968) "Standardization: a technique to control for extraneous variables." Applied Statistics 23: 118-136.
LIEBERSON, S. (1978) "A reconsideration of the income differences found between migrants and Northern-born blacks." Amer. J. of Sociology 83: 940-966.
LITTLE, R.J.A. (1978) "Models for cross-classified data from the World Fertility Survey." Technical Bulletin No. 5, World Fertility Survey.
NELDER, J. A. and R.W.M. WEDDERBURN (1972) "Generalized linear models." J. of the Royal Statistical Society, Series A 135: 370-384.
PULLUM, T. W. (1978) "Standardization." Statistical Bulletin No. 4, World Fertility Survey.
ROSENBERG, M. (1962) "Test factor standardization as a method of interpretation." Social Forces 41: 53-61.

Roderick J. A. Little completed his Ph.D. dissertation at Imperial College, University of London, and was for two years Research Associate at the University of Chicago. Since 1976 he has been a statistician with the World Fertility Survey, London. His research interests include multivariate analysis with incomplete data and log-linear models.

Thomas W. Pullum is Director of the Center for Studies in Demography and Ecology at the University of Washington. His interests include fertility and occupational mobility. He worked with the World Fertility Survey in London in 1976-1977, when much of the work leading to the present article was done.

AGGREGATION BIAS

An Empirical Demonstration

7

JEANNE E. MOORMAN

University of Wisconsin

> One cannot argue on principle against the statement that indi-
> vidual correlation and ecological correlation will usually not
> coincide—but neither can one rest with such an observation.
>
> —Scheuch (1966: 152)

Any discussion of aggregation bias necessarily begins with
Robinson's (1950) well-known article "Ecological Correlation
and the Behavior of Individuals." Since that article, there has
been considerable discussion of the ecological fallacy, but little

AUTHOR'S NOTE: *This research was supported by Public Health Service Train-
ing Grant NIGMS-GM01190 and a National Research Service Award Training
Grant 1 T32 HD07014 as well as by the facilities of the Center for Demography and
Ecology at the University of Wisconsin—Madison with funds provided by the
National Institute of Child Health and Human Development Grant 1 P01 HD05876.
I would like to thank Halliman H. Winsborough for his assistance and direction. I
would also like to thank Barbara Witt and Barbara Aldrich for their help in the
preparation of extracts from the Public Use Sample tapes and the Census Sum-
mary Tapes.*

attempt to actually measure the amount of bias introduced by aggregation of individuals into areal units when data existed at both levels.

Scheuch (1966: 152) did posit two highly relevant questions in his discourse on the ecological fallacy:

1. What factors determine the difference between the two correlations?
2. How important will this difference be in a concrete case?

However, he regrettably finds little evidence that either question has been the target of research in the area. Both Allardt (1969) and Hannan (1970) as well as Scheuch (1969) and others regret that the inference complication originally described by Robinson seems to have slowed research in some areas that lack individual data. Hannan (1970: 475) states: "The establishment of a more sophisticated methodology would seem to require movement from such categorical thinking to a consideration of likely magnitude of errors and consequent faulty inference associated with specified procedures under a variety of situations."

The release of the 1960 and 1970 Public Use Samples provides an opportunity to determine the extent of bias in correlation coefficients at several aggregate levels.

The subsequent analysis examines whether aggregation at the census tract level results in significant inflation of the correlation between certain variables related to fertility behavior, and if so, whether the inflation occurs in a systematic way. If such bias is both significant and systematic, faulty inferences can be avoided while the aggregate level data could still be exploited to some extent. If the bias introduced by aggregation should prove nonsignificant, aggregate level fertility data can be used in place of individual data in similar contexts.

ANALYSIS OF COVARIANCE

An analysis of covariance framework has been recommended for use in examining the relationship between ecological correlation and individual correlation by several persons including Schuessler (1969), Duncan, Cuzzort, and Duncan (1961), as well as Robinson himself (1950).

The specific method of analysis used here includes multiple regression adaptation of analysis of covariance discussed in detail by Bogue and Harris (1954). It is necessary to use an indirect method of obtaining the within-group sums of squares and cross-products because limitations in the individual level data prevent identification of group membership. In order to secure the required values for the usual analysis of covariance table, three steps are required. First, records for each individual are entered into a regression equation to provide total sums of squares and cross-products. Then records for the groups (tracts) are used in a weighted regression to provide between-group values. Finally, within-group values are secured by subtraction.

SAMPLE

The Public Use Sample of one in 100 households for 1970 provides data for the individual level analysis. Because this sample does not identify geographic location of the individual for areas of less than 250,000, it is not possible to assign actual tract locations to individuals. Consequently, the Census Summary Tapes are used to ascertain the between-group values necessary for the analysis of covariance. The tract values are entered in a weighted regression program, the weights determined by the size of the tract and a function of the total number of individual records extracted from the Public Use Sample. The sample area is restricted to the Chicago-Gary-Hammond-East Chicago Standard Consolidated Area (SCA) to maintain manageable dimensions and to eliminate possible regional and rural-urban differences. The sample is further restricted to the white population. These restrictions serve to lessen the possibility of violating an analysis of covariance assumption of equal within-group regression coefficients (b_{yxb}). Again, because individual records cannot be identified as to group membership, this assumption cannot be tested during analysis. As race, residence, and region have been identified as variables relevant to fertility, holding them constant by restricting the sample is more likely to ensure equal within-group regression coefficients for the remaining variables under consideration.

VARIABLES

The use of two different although related data sources limits the choice of variables available. Therefore, only four independent variables are included in this analysis. For each woman in the Public Use Sample, age, marital status, number of years of education completed, and labor force participation can be ascertained with little difficulty. However, restrictions on the exact form of each variable arise from the available cross-tabulations in the summary tapes.

A commonly used fertility measure (and the only one available from aggregate census data) is the child-woman ratio. The usual age ranges for this ratio are children 0-4 to women 15-49. The age range for children could be limited to children under three to reduce the mortality bias present in this indirect fertility measure.[1] Therefore, two forms of this ratio are considered as dependent variables. The age range for women will also be restricted to women 15-44 because of similar limits on the independent variables as available from the Summary Tapes.[2] Own children under three and own children under five of individual women 15-44 will be considered comparable to the ratios of all children under three and under five to women 15-44 in the tracts, and shall be referred to as C/WR3 and C/WR5 respectively.

In summary, then, from the Public Use Sample for individual women aged 15-44, the variables are:

Age: 15-44
Marital status: Dummy variable
Education: Scale of 1-4
Labor force: Dummy variable
C/WR3: Number of own children under three
C/WR5: Number of own children under five

and for tracts, from the Census Summary Tapes:

Age: Average age of women 15-44
Marital status: Percent of women 15-44 ever married
Education: Average value of 1-4 scale
Labor force: Percent of women 15-44 in the labor force
C/WR3: All children under 3 to women 15-44
C/WR5: All children under 5 to women 15-44.

Table 1 shows means and standard deviations for the six variables. Aggregation and weighting has had little effect on the mean values across the two levels. However, as expected, the standard deviation has decreased considerably at the aggregate tract level.

ANALYSIS OF VARIANCE—C/WR5

After weighting to force equal sample sizes at the two levels, an analysis of variance table can be constructed from the results of the separate level regression analysis. Consider first the results from the regression of the C/WR5 (see Table 2). In this composite analysis the Public Use Sample (PUS) of 12,608 individual records is unweighted and provides a total sum of squared variation of 6,285. The between-group sum of squares is derived from a weighted regression of the tract level data. Surprisingly, this results in a nonsignificant F ratio between the two estimates of mean square error, implying no significant bias in the analysis at the group level.

It can be argued, however, that the mean square error for the between-group sum of squares is not appropriate, because of the weighting by a factor of approximately .001 of the size of the tract rather than the actual number in each tract. Consider, therefore, the result if an alternate weighting process is undertaken. In Table 3, the tract level data is weighted by the actual number in each tract, and, consequently, each record in the PUS sample is weighted by a factor of approximately 100 to achieve

TABLE 1
Summary Statistics, Chicago SCA, 1970

Variable	Individual		Tract	
	mean	s.d.	mean	s.d.
1. C/WR3	.232	.501	.235	.069
2. C/WR5	.395	.706	.339	.109
3. Age	28.3	8.74	28.3	1.03
4. Education	2.80	.922	2.80	.349
5. Marital Status	.680	.466	.678	.098
6. Labor force part.	.465	.500	.466	.097

the desired equal sample sizes. As a result of this weighting, the sums of squares for each level are inflated by approximately a factor of 100, while the degrees of freedom associated with each necessarily remain the same. Consequently, the mean square error estimates also reflect the inflation factor and the F ratio value remains unchanged.

Strictly speaking, neither of these two tables reflects true comparison of the ratios of actual estimates of the mean square error. In the first table the weighting process on the between-group estimate artificially deflates the sum of squares while leaving the degrees of freedom unaffected. Likewise, in the second table, the total sum of squares (and subsequently the within-sum of squares) has been inflated artificially, while the degrees of freedom remain unchanged. Consider what would result if, instead of a one in 100 sample, we had the entire population from which to measure the total sum of squares (see Table 4). The total sum of squares shown in Table 3 might be reasonably close to the actual value, but the degrees of freedom would be considerably different for the total and within groups. The estimate of the between group mean square error shown in Table 3, along with the associated sum of squares and degrees of freedom, can be considered to reflect the appropriate relationship. The resulting F ratio in this case is most significant.

Another way of looking at this seeming paradox is to accept as the "correct" estimate of the mean square error for between groups the figure 10.3 appearing in Table 3, for which the sum of squares

TABLE 2
C/WR5 Analysis of Variance

Source	Sum of squares	Degrees of freedom	Mean square	F ratio
Between groups[1]	151	1,473	.103	.187
Within groups	6,134	11,134	.551	
Total[2]	6,285	12,607		

1. Summary tapes each tract weighted by $n_j/100.59$? n_j = number of women 15-44 in each tract.
2. PUS unweighted, N = 12,608

is appropriately weighted by n_j (the number in each group) and is associated with the appropriate degrees of freedom. Then, accept the mean square error within groups that results from an appropriately unweighted sum of squares and correct degrees of freedom found in Table 2—specifically, the value .551. Combining these two "correct" estimates of the mean square error produces, again, a significant F ratio.[3] One must conclude, on the basis of these considerations, that significant statistical bias exists in the analysis under consideration here. However, considering that the power of this test relies on the large sample size, excessive concern with the statistical significance is largely unwarranted.

Turning now to the regression of C/WR3, a similar argument follows. The effects of the two alternate weighting processes on the sum of squares for each of the levels both produce nonsignificant F ratios. Theoretical approximations for the total and within group sums of squares, given knowledge of the entire population, are shown in Table 5. This process, as before, inflates the F ratio by a factor of 100 and consequently indicates that significant statistical bias is introduced by the aggregation process.

On the basis of these results, it would appear that some degree of bias exists in these two measures of fertility at an aggregate level (although the statistical significance of the bias is questionable because of the power of the tests involved). There is no reason to believe that the independent variables do not manifest

TABLE 3
C/WR5 Analysis of Variance: Alternate Weighting

Source	Sum of squares	Degrees of freedom	Mean square	F ratio
Between groups[1]	15,152	1,473	10.3	.186
Within groups	617,010	11,134	55.4	
Total[2]	632,162	12,607		

1. Summary tapes weighted by n.
2. PUS weighted by a factor of 100.59

similar amounts of bias. However, on the principle that identification of the degree of bias in each variable and the interaction of that bias with the bias in other variables may prove useful in similar processes, further examination of both the correlation and regression coefficients is undertaken. Both C/WR3 and C/WR5 are again considered in the event that one may prove less biased than the other.

A cursory look at the F ratios for between and within mean squares for each of the independent variables supports the prior conclusion of significant aggregation bias in all the variables if one follows a similar argument as was presented for the two child/woman ratio variables and inflates each F ratio by a factor of approximately 100 (see Table 6). The smallest value of an inflated ratio would be 10.6, indicating that considerable bias is introduced at an aggregate level into any summary statistic that is a function of the variance of the variable.

The usual statistic referred to when considering aggregation bias is, of course, the correlation coefficient. Examination of the correlations among the six variables in most cases supports the prior conclusion of considerable bias. Take, for example, r_{14} (Table 6), the correlation between C/WR3 and marital status. The total correlation (r_t) is .31, while the between group or ecological correlation (r_b) is .69, an obviously significant difference. However, consider r_{35}; the difference between the total and ecological correlation in this case is only .02. The decision here is not quite so clear. Tests for the difference between two correlations are not appropriate since two independent samples are

TABLE 4
C/WR5 Analysis of Variance: Hypothetical

Source	Sum of squares	Degrees of freedom	Mean square	F ratio
Between groups	15,152	1.473	10.3	21.4
Within groups	617,010	1,259,326	.48	
Total	632,162	1,260,799		

not involved here. One could ask whether or not a value observed for the ecological correlation could have been observed at the individual level. In other words, does the confidence interval around the total correlation include the value of the ecological correlation? Unfortunately, in no case does this situation actually occur, undoubtedly because of the large sample's producing extremely narrow intervals. One again concludes that there is significant bias in each observed between-group or ecological correlation.

Robinson (1950) originally formulated a relationship between the total between- and within-correlations that is dependent on what he terms correlation ratios. Duncan et al. (1961) and Hannan (1970) have since continued to use these ratios in their subsequent discussions of ecological correlations. These ratios are simply the percent of total sum of squares that is delegated to the between-group component; i.e.:

$$N_x^2 = \frac{\sum_j n_j (\overline{X}_j - \overline{X})^2}{\sum_{ij}\sum (x_{ij} - \overline{X})^2} \qquad [1]$$

Robinson then defines the relation between the three correlations as:

$$r_t = N_x N_y r_b + \sqrt{1 - N_x^2} \sqrt{1 - N_y^2} \, r_w \qquad [2]$$

TABLE 5
C/WR5 Analysis of Variance: Hypothetical

Source	Sum of squares	Degrees of freedom	Mean square	F ratio
Between groups	5,956	1,473	4.04	16.3
Within groups	311,916	1,259,326	.248	
Total	318,872	1,260,799		

He further states that the ecological correlation will equal the total correlation when the average within-area correlation is not less than the total correlation. That is, when:

$$r_w = kr_t \text{ where } k = \frac{1 - N_x N_y}{\sqrt{1 - N_x^2} \sqrt{1 - N_y^2}} \quad [3]$$

with k always greater than or equal to 1.

In this form the relation between the correlations does not appear to be intuitively obvious. If one were to consider an additional correlation ratio for the cross-product sum of squares, N_{xy}, it can be shown that:

$$r_t = \frac{N_x N_y}{N_{xy}} r_b, \text{ or } r_b = \frac{N_{xy}}{N_x N_y} r_t \quad [4]$$

and,

$$r_t = \frac{\sqrt{1 - N_x^2} \sqrt{1 - N_y^2}}{1 - N_{xy}} r_w \quad [5]$$

and therefore:

$$r_t = \frac{N_x N_y}{2N_{xy}} r_b + \frac{\sqrt{1 - N_x^2} \sqrt{1 - N_y^2}}{2(1 - N_{xy})} r_w. \quad [6]$$

In this alternate form, the ecological correlation will quite obviously equal the total correlation when $N_{xy} / N_x N_y$ is equal to

TABLE 6
Sums of Squares, Sums of Cross-Products, and Zero Order Correlations, Chicago SCA, 1970

	C/WR3 (1)	C/WR5 (2)	Age (3)	Marital Status (4)	Education (5)	Labor Force Partic. (6)	1970
1. C/WR3							
Between*	59.21	.92	.07	.69	-.52	-.31	r_b
Within	3110.67	.83	-.04	.30	.08	-.27	r_w
Total**	3169.88	.83	-.04	.31	.05	-.27	r_t
F		.1430					
N_{xy}	.0187						
2. C/WR5							
Between	87.08	150.60	.20	.75	-.52	-.46	r_b
Within	3612.61	6133.62	.01	.37	.08	-.30	r_w
Total	3699.69	6284.22	.02	.38	.04	-.31	r_t
F			.1870				
N_{xy}	.0235	.0240					
3. Age							
Between	65.65	287.23	13372.23	.46	.09	-.34	r_b
Within	-2276.90	1136.40	950708.89	.60	.11	.01	r_w
Total	-2211.25	1423.63	964081.12	.60	.11	.01	r_t
F				.1060			
N_{xy}	-.0297	.2018					
4. Marital Status							
Between	58.43	100.93	589.22	120.29	-.31	-.40	r_b
Within	859.12	1466.36	30141.14	2623.01	.14	-.15	r_w
Total	917.55	1567.31	30730.36	2743.30	.10	-.16	r_t
F					.3470		
N_{xy}	.0637	.0644	.0192	.0438			
5. Education							
Between	-155.29	-251.32	407.39	-132.83	1535.49	.17	r_b
Within	438.80	574.00	10382.03	684.13	9186.77	.14	r_w
Total	283.51	322.68	10789.40	551.30	10722.26	.14	r_t
F			.0378			1.263	
N_{xy}	-.5477	-.7789	.0378	-.2409	.1432		
6. Labor Force							
Between	-26.33	-61.68	-433.97	-47.83	72.14	118.47	r_b
Within	-822.64	-1293.33	793.06	-431.95	753.91	3018.17	r_w
Total	-848.97	-1355.01	359.09	-479.78	826.05	3136.64	r_t
F						.2970	
N_{xy}	.0310	.0455	-1.2085	.0997	.0873	.0378	

*Summary tapes weighted by $n_j/100.59$

**Public Use Sample unweighted
Diagonal—sums of squares
Below diagonal—sums of cross-products
Above diagonal—zero order correlations

Degree of freedom—between   1,473
within   11,134
total   12,607

one, or, in other words, when the proportion of the sum of squares delegated to the between-group component of the cross-product (N_{xy}) is equal to the product of the square roots of the same proportion in each sum of squares ($N_x N_y$). That is, of course, precisely the relation that exists in the three components of the correlation coefficient.

The ratio $N_{xy}/N_x N_y$, then, is simply the proportionate adjustment of the total correlation that results in the observed value for the ecological correlation. If the ratio is greater than 1 or less than -1, r_b is greater than r_t in absolute value, if it is between -1 and 1, r_b is less than r_t in absolute value while a negative value indicates a change of sign between the total and ecological correlations.

The question that immediately arises is: how frequently will it in fact be the case that the ratio $N_{xy}/N_x N_y$ approximates unity? Table 7 shows values for the ratio for the two dependent and four independent variables being considered here. In the four cases where the two correlations (r_t and r_b) are within 10 units of one another, the ratio varies between .846 and 1.187. Unfortunately, the ratio does not vary directly with the absolute differences between the total and ecological correlations since it is a function of the size of r_t. One cannot say, then, that the closer $N_{xy}/N_x N_y$ is to unity, the closer the ecological correlation will be to the total correlation in absolute value. Take, for example, r_{23} and r_{64}, with corresponding ratios of 11.049 and 2.450 respectively. The absolute difference between the total and ecological correlations for r_{23} is .18 and for r_{64} is .24. All that can be concluded is that the ecological correlation for r_{23} is more biased relative to its total than that for r_{64}.

Of the fifteen total correlations presented, only four have ecological correlations within 20% of their respective total correlations (ratios between .80 and 1.20). Another four ecological correlations differ from their respective totals by a factor of 10 or greater, and a total of five have opposite signs. This appears to be overwhelming evidence of the unreliability of correlations at the aggregate level of analysis relative to their corresponding individual level correlations.

Blalock (1961: 112) has claimed that, in certain circumstances, the regression coefficient is less biased than the correlation coefficient. Let us consider to what extent this is true in the

TABLE 7
Bias in Zero Order Correlations, Chicago SCA, 1970

Variable	C/WR3 1.	C/WR5 2.	Age 3.	Marital Status 4.	Ed. 5.	Labor Force 6.
1. C/WR3		1.11	-1.84	2.23	-10.58	1.17
2. C/WR5	.83		11.05	1.99	-13.29	1.51
3. Age	-.04	.02		.78	.85	-52.72
4. Marital status	.31	.38	.60		-3.04	2.45
5. Education	.05	.04	.11	.10		1.19
6. Labor force	-.27	-.31	.01	-.16	.14	

Upper diagonal $N_{xy}/N_x N_y$
Lower diagonal r_t; $r_b = (N_{xy}/N_x N_y)\, r_t$

present data. In Blalock's case, when grouping by geographical proximity approached the effect of grouping to maximize the variation in the independent variable, the aggregate regression coefficient was less biased than the correlation.

It can be shown that:

$$b_{yxt} = (N_x^2/N_{xy})(b_{yxb}) \qquad [7]$$

or conversely:

$$b_{yxb} = (N_{xy}/N_x^2)(b_{yxt}) \qquad [8]$$

and therefore:

$$b_{yxb} = (N_{xy}/N_x)(r_t)(\sqrt{C_{yyt}} / \sqrt{C_{xxb}}) \qquad [9]$$

whereas:

$$r_{xyb} = (N_{xy}/N_x)(r_t)(\sqrt{C_{yyt}} / \sqrt{C_{yyb}}). \qquad [10]$$

It can be readily seen that the only difference between the ecological correlation and ecological regression coefficients is the difference in the between-group sum of squares for the dependent and independent variables, C_{xxb} and C_{yyb}. This difference will depend considerably on the scales of the two variables. The ecological regression coefficient can, therefore, be more biased relative to the total correlation than the ecological correlation coefficient whenever C_{xxb} is less than C_{yyb} and the usual relation between the total and ecological correlation holds (r_b greater than r_t).

Conventionally, one will be more interested in the bias in the ecological regression coefficient relative to the individual regression coefficient rather than relative to the total correlation. In this case we are concerned with the quantity N_{xy}/N_x^2 relative to N_{xy}/N_xN_y. In Table 8 the values of the two ratios are shown for the four independent variables with each dependent variable. In the first column, representing the regression of C/WR3 on each of the independent variables separately, the between-group regression coefficients for age and labor force participation are slightly more biased than the corresponding correlation coefficients, while those for education and marital status are considerably less biased. None of the ratios is close enough to unity to consider the ecological coefficients adequate replacements for the individual level coefficients.

In the second column the dependent variable is C/WR5. Here, three of the four between-group regression coefficients can be considered better estimates of the total coefficients than the corresponding correlations. The closest estimate is the between-group regression coefficient for labor force participation (-.521) which is 20% higher in absolute value than its corresponding individual level coefficient. Only one coefficient, that for education, has a ratio that indicates a sign change at the aggregate level. Clearly, none of the aggregate coefficients can be considered adequate replacements for the individual level coefficients.

Blalock (1961) has also suggested that analysis at the aggregate level may, in effect, be controlling for the influence of other variables. If this is in fact the case, higher order partial corre-

TABLE 8
Zero Order Correlations and Regression Coefficients,
Chicago SCA, 1970

Independent Variables	Dependent Variables			
	C/WR3		C/WR5	
	r_{xy}	b_{yx}	r_{xy}	b_{yx}
Age				
Between	.07	.005	.20	.021
Total	-.04	-.002	.02	.001
Ratio	-1.84	-2.14	11.05	14.52
Marital Status				
Between	.69	.486	.75	.839
Total	.31	.334	.38	.571
Ratio	2.23	1.45	1.99	1.47
Education				
Between	-.52	-.101	-.52	-.164
Total	.05	.026	.04	.030
Ratio	-10.58	-3.83	-13.29	-5.44
Labor Force Partic.				
Between	-.31	-.222	-.46	-.521
Total	-.27	-.271	-.31	-.432
Ratio	1.17	.82	1.51	1.20

Ratio for $r = N_{xy}/N_x N_y$
Ratio for $b = N_{xy}/N_x^2$

lations at the aggregate level may control for the remaining influence. Comparison of these higher order aggregate level partials with similarly partialed individual level coefficients should show less bias than the zero order coefficients.

At the first order partial correlation and regression, and at each higher order level, the algebra for sorting out the components of bias in the ecological correlations becomes successively more cumbersome. For example, for the first order partial correlation:

$$r_{xy \cdot z_t} = \cfrac{\cfrac{C_{xy_t}}{\sqrt{C_{xx_t}}\sqrt{C_{yy_t}}}}{\cfrac{C_{xy_b}}{\sqrt{C_{xx_b}}\sqrt{C_{yy_b}}}} \cdot \cfrac{\cfrac{C_{xz_t}C_{yz_t}}{C_{zz_t}\sqrt{C_{xx_t}C_{yy_t}}}}{\cfrac{C_{xz_b}C_{yz_b}}{C_{zz_b}\sqrt{C_{xx_b}C_{yy_b}}}} \cdot \cfrac{\sqrt{1 - \cfrac{C_{xz_b}^2}{C_{xx_b}C_{zz_b}}}\sqrt{1 - \cfrac{C_{yz_b}^2}{C_{yy_b}C_{zz_b}}}}{\sqrt{1 - \cfrac{C_{xz_t}^2}{C_{xx_t}C_{zz_t}}}\sqrt{1 - \cfrac{C_{yz_t}}{C_{yy_t}C_{zz_t}}}} r_{xy \cdot z_b} \qquad [11]$$

Rather than try to sort out the above relation for each variable combination, I will make use of the simple fact that:

$$\frac{r_b}{r_t} = \frac{N_{xy}}{N_x N_y} \text{ and } \frac{b_b}{b_t} = \frac{N_{xy}}{N_x^2} \qquad [12]$$

and generalize to each higher order.

Referring back to Table 8, it seems that the two "best," i.e., least biased, zero order ecological regression coefficients are those for marital status and labor force participation. The ratios for these two variables indicate no sign change between the ecological and total correlation and regression coefficients and show ratio values relatively close to unity. If the marital status and labor force variables are entered simultaneously into regression equations for each dependent variable, however, the respective ratios indicate an increase in the proportion of bias in both partial correlations and regression coefficients compared with the zero-order ratios for both the marital status and labor force variables in the equation for C/WR3, and in the regression coefficient for the labor force variable in the equation for C/WR5 (Table 9). Although the coefficients for marital status in the C/WR5 equation have changed considerably from the zero order coefficients, their relative differences remain the same: 1.99 for the correlations and 1.47 for the regression coefficients. The partial correlations for C/WR5 and labor force participation controlling for marital status is unbiased, having the same value for both ecological and total levels.

If we consider all possible two-variable equations (Table 9), a pattern emerges based on the sign and size of the bias at the zero order. Classifying the bias at the zero order as positive or negative and large (greater than 2.5 in absolute value) or small (less than 2.5) and comparing different combinations of these classifications produce rather interesting results. For example, combining age and labor force variables in an equation for C/WR3 combines small positive and negative biases and results in bias ratios at the first order that are closer to unity for both partial correlations and regression coefficients. A similar result is seen in the equation for the regression of C/WR3 on age and marital status. Here, the regression coefficients at the ecological level are remarkably similar to those for the total regression. However, combining two variables that have positive small biases at the zero order (marital status and labor force participation) has the mixed result discussed above. Combining a variable with large positive bias with one with small positive bias (age and labor force participation or age and marital status) in the equation for C/WR5 also reduces the bias ratios over all coefficients relative to the zero order ratios but the rather large biases in the zero order coefficients for age with C/WR5 are not nearly compensated for.

Combining a variable with large negative bias with one small positive bias at the zero order produces bias ratios closer to unity for the variable that originally had small bias (see marital status and education or labor force and education) with only one exception, the regression coefficient for the labor force variable with education held constant in the equation for C/WR3. The large negative bias ratio for the education variable increased in absolute value in the equations with marital status and declined in those with labor force participation, but remained negative. Combination of two negative or two large biases (age and education) has either little effect or makes the bias ratios considerably removed from unity. It appears that the use of the education variable has only deleterious effects on the coefficients of the other variables in the aggregate level equations.

TABLE 9
First Order Partial Correlations and Regression
Coefficients, Chicago SCA, 1970

Independent Variables	Dependent Variables				Zero Order Bias	
	C/WR3		C/WR5		C/WR3	C/WR5
	$r_{xy.1}$	$b_{yx.1}$	$r_{xy.1}$	$b_{yx.1}$		
Age						
Between	−.04	−.003	.05	.005		
Total	−.04	−.002	.02	.002	negative small	positive large
Ratio	.98	1.19	2.45	3.17		
Labor Force Partic.						
Between	−.31	−.232	−.43	−.502		
Total	−.27	−.270	−.31	−.432	positive small	positive small
Ratio	1.15	.86	1.40	1.16		
Age						
Between	.14	.008	.29	.027		
Total	−.05	−.003	.01	.001	negative small	positive large
Ratio	−3.10	−3.09	20.68	23.2		
Education						
Between	−.53	−.103	−.55	−.171		
Total	.05	.029	.04	.029	negative large	negative large
Ratio	−9.87	−3.55	−14.75	−5.90		
	$r_{xy.1}$	$b_{yx.1}$	$r_{xy.1}$	$b_{yx.1}$		
Age						
Between	−.39	−.021	−.25	−.020		
Total	−.29	−.020	−.28	−.026	negative small	positive large
Ratio	1.31	1.04	.89	.76		
Marital Status						
Between	.75	.589	.76	.936		
Total	.42	.560	.46	.863	positive small	positive small
Ratio	1.78	1.05	1.65	1.08		

TABLE 9 (Continued)

Independent Variables	Dependent Variables				Zero Order Bias	
	C/WR3		C/WR5		C/WR3	C/WR5
Marital Status						
Between	.65	.473	.70	.753		
Total	.28	.295	.35	.509	positive small	positive small
Ratio	2.32	1.60	1.99	1.48		
Labor Force Partic.						
Between	-.06	-.031	-.27	-.217		
Total	-.23	-.226	-.27	-.354	positive small	positive small
Ratio	.24	.14	1.00	.61		
	$r_{xy.1}$	$b_{yx.1}$	$r_{xy.1}$	$b_{yx.1}$		
Marital Status						
Between	.65	.414	.73	.728		
Total	.131	.333	.38	.571	positive small	positive small
Ratio	2.12	1.24	1.93	1.27		
Education						
Between	-.44	-.065	-.46	-.101		
Total	.02	.009	.001	.001	negative large	negative large
Ratio	-24.37	-6.98	-462.3	-137.9		
Education						
Between	-.49	-.093	-.51	-.143		
Total	.09	.048	.09	.065	negative large	negative large
Ratio	-5.41	-1.93	-5.79	-2.22		
Labor Force Partic.						
Between	-.27	-.165	-.44	-.433		
Total	-.28	-.283	-.31	-.449	positive small	positive small
Ratio	.96	.58	1.41	.97		

Ratio for $r = \dfrac{r_b}{r_t}$

Ratio for $b = \dfrac{b_b}{b_t}$

Let us now consider the possible second order combinations of variables in regression equations for C/WR3 and C/WR5 (Table 10). Adding labor force participation to age and marital status in the equation for C/WR3 has resulted in bias ratios more removed from unity for the coefficients for labor force relative to its zero-order bias ratio and increased the bias ratio in the coefficients for age and marital status relative to their first order combination. The aggregate coefficient for labor force and age are also worse relative to their first-order combination while those for marital status and labor force are better. One concludes that introducing a third variable with relatively small bias into an equation that has already balanced biases tends to worsen the bias in all three variables. Age and marital status did not balance each other quite so well in the first order equation, because of the large positive bias ratio between age and C/WR5. In this case, introducing a third variable results in bias ratios closer to unity for all three regression coefficients relative to their zero order biases and relative to the bias in regression coefficients of all combinations of first order equations, with the minor exception of marital status. In the first order equation for the regression of C/WR5 on age and marital status, the marital status regression coefficient is slightly less biased than that coefficient in the second-order equation for C/WR5 age, marital status, and labor force participation; however, the difference is minor (1.08 versus 1.10).

Using the education variable in a second order equation in most cases decreases its own bias and is inconsistent in increasing or decreasing the bias in the other two variables. For the most part, it increases bias in the regression coefficients and decreases that in the partial correlations. None of the aggregate level second order equations can be considered relatively "good" as a replacement for the individual level equation since the biases in the regression coefficients are never close to unity for all the variables in the equation when eduction is one of the variables being considered.

In summary, then, if one desired the "best" regression equation possible at the aggregate level (where "best" refers to bias ratios close to unity for each variable in the equation), one could consider the first order equation for the regression of C/WR3 on age and marital status and the second order equation for the regression of C/WR5 on age, marital status, and labor force participation. The biases in the regression coefficients for the equation for C/WR3 are 5% or less while the biases for the C/WR5 equation are slightly worse, varying between 7% and 14%. For the most part, the aggregate regression coefficients are less biased relative to the individual level coefficients than are the correlation coefficients. At the zero order, 63% of the ecological regression coefficients are less biased than are the respective correlations and at the first and second order, 21% are less biased.

In order to see if any of these generalizations are valid in other situations or merely artifacts of the particular data involved, the preceding analysis was duplicated at a slightly larger aggregate level. Individual records from the Public Use Sample for 1970 were selected from the two states, Illinois and Indiana, which contain the Chicago SCA. Again, from the Census Summary Tapes, average values for the six variables were obtained at the county level. The mean values and standard deviations for the six variables at each level, individual and county, are close, but not quite so close as those between individual and tract level data, while the standard deviations decline even further at the county level than they do at the tract level. The correlation ratios for each variable indicate that, in general, tract ratios are closer to unity than corresponding county ratios. However, in four cases, labor force with C/WR3, C/WR5, and age, and marital status with age, the ecological correlation at the county level is closer to its corresponding total correlation than is the tract level ecological correlation. Two of these four ecological correlations, those for labor force with C/WR3 and age with marital status, are within 15% of their respective total correlations; and one, labor force with C/WR5, reproduces its total correlation exactly. However, the remaining eleven cases have considerably worse ecological correlations than those between the same variables at the tract level of analysis.

TABLE 10
Second Order Partial Correlations and Regression
Coefficients, Chicago SCA, 1970

Independent Variable	Dependent Variable			
	C/WR3		C/WR5	
	$r_{xy.12}$	$b_{yx.12}$	$r_{xy.12}$	$b_{yx.12}$
Age				
Between	-.41	-.022	-.32	-.025
Total	-.28	-.018	-.26	-.023
Ratio	1.48	1.22	1.25	1.07
Marital Status				
Between	.72	.566	.73	.855
Total	.38	.507	.42	.776
Ratio	1.87	1.12	1.73	1.10
Labor Force Partic.				
Between	-.15	-.076	-.33	-.266
Total	-.20	-.191	-.24	-.311
Ratio	.71	.40	1.37	.86
	$r_{xy.12}$	$b_{yx.12}$	$r_{xy.12}$	$b_{yx.12}$
Age				
Between	-.31	-.016	-.14	-.010
Total	-.30	-.020	-.28	-.026
Ratio	1.04	.77	.51	.40
Marital Status				
Between	.69	.503	.70	.788
Total	.42	.558	.46	.861
Ratio	1.65	.90	1.54	.91
Education				
Between	-.37	-.053	-.42	-.093
Total	.04	.018	.02	.012
Ratio	-10.24	-2.98	-24.01	-7.78

TABLE 10 (Continued)

Independent Variable	Dependent Variable			
	C/WR3		C/WR5	
	$r_{xy.12}$	$b_{yx.12}$	$r_{xy.12}$	$b_{yx.12}$
Age				
Between	.05	.003	.16	.014
Total	-.05	-.003	.01	.001
Ratio	-.94	-1.01	12.97	14.75
Labor Force Partic.				
Between	-.24	-.154	-.38	-.379
Total	-.28	-.284	-.31	-.449
Ratio	.84	.54	1.20	.85
Education				
Between	-.49	-.095	-.52	-.150
Total	.10	.051	.09	.064
Ratio	-5.14	-1.85	-6.09	-2.35
	$r_{xy.12}$	$b_{yx.12}$	$r_{xy.12}$	$b_{yx.12}$
Marital Status				
Between	.62	.407	.67	.652
Total	.27	.287	.34	.501
Ratio	2.27	1.41	1.97	1.30
Labor Force Partic.				
Between	-.04	-.018	-.27	-.918
Total	-.24	-.235	-.27	-.364
Ratio	.15	.08	1.01	2.52
Education				
Between	-.44	-.065	-.47	-.098
Total	.06	-.030	.05	.032
Ratio	-7.52	-2.19	-10.02	-3.03

Ratio for $r = \dfrac{r_b}{r_t}$

Ratio for $b = \dfrac{b_b}{b_t}$

Turning again to the regression framework, the aggregate regression coefficients for marital status are considerably less biased at the county level than they were at the tract level. However, those for age are considerably more biased at the county level. The bias ratios for eduction and labor force variables at the county level are somewhat similar to those at the tract level. At both the tract and county level a similar downward trend in thebias ratio at the first order over the zero order has occurred in spite of change in the size and sign of the age zero order bias ratio at the county level of analysis.

However, none of the aggregate two-variable equations has proved an adequate replacement for the individual level regression equation at the county level, and in only one of the three variable equations is an aggregate regression coefficient an acceptable substitute for the individual level coefficient. While it appears that the bias ratios balance each other out in similar patterns at both the tract and county levels, the relatively large bias ratios at the county level seem to prevent higher order equations with acceptable aggregate coefficients.

SUMMARY

Although considerable aggregation bias exists in each of the six variables, when grouped at the census tract level, adequate regression equations can be obtained for each of the two dependent variables. The interplay of the bias factors seems to cancel each other out for certain combinations of variables, producing aggregate level regression coefficients that are within 15% or less of the corresponding individual level regression coefficients. This result was not found to extend to aggregation into fewer groups with larger numbers of individuals per group, specifically at the county level.

While it is usually true that aggregate level regression coefficients are less biased than aggregate level correlation coefficients, it is not the rule since exceptions can be found at each order of correlation and regression. Furthermore, it has been shown that ecological correlation for larger groups (counties) are not necessarily more biased than those for smaller aggregates (tracts).

IMPLICATIONS

The generalizability of these results to areas other than those investigated is questionable to say the least. Replication of the analysis for other tracted areas is indicated before assuming the relationship between any of the variables will hold for any area other than the 1970 Chicago SCA. The main point illustrated here is the unpredictability of the direction and size of the difference between ecological and individual coefficients. Although the patterns found at the tract level seem to hold at the county level of aggregation, it is impossible to predict the size of the ecological correlation or that combination of variables that will balance out the bias in the ecological coefficients without undertaking as extensive an analysis as done here. This conclusion serves to further strengthen the arguments against the use of the ecological correlation as a measure of association.

NOTES

1. For an extensive discussion of the sources of bias in census fertility estimates, see Rindfuss (1974).

2. For a more extensive discussion of the compromises resulting in the final form of each variable, refer to Moorman (1977).

3. $F = 18.7$; 1,473 and 11,134 degrees of freedom.

REFERENCES

ALLARDT, E. (1969) "Aggregate analysis: the problem of its informative value," pp. 41-52 in M. Dogan and S. Rokkan (eds.) Social Ecology. Cambridge: M.I.T. Press.

BLALOCK, H. M., Jr. (1961) Causal Inferences in Non-experimental Research. Chapel Hill: Univ. of North Carolina Press.

BOGUE, D. and D. L. HARRIS (1954) Comparative Population and Urban Research via Multiple Regression and Covariance Analysis. Oxford, OH: Scripps Foundation for Research in Population Problems.

DUNCAN, O. D., R. CUZZORT and B. DUNCAN (1961) Statistical Geography. Glencoe, IL: Free Press.

HAMMOND, J. L. (1973) "Two sources of error in ecological correlations." Amer. Soc. Rev. 38: 764-777.

HANNAN, M. (1971) "Problems of aggregation," pp. 473-508 in Blalock (ed.) Causal Models in the Social Sciences. Chicago, IL: Aldine.

———— (1970) "Problems of aggregation and disaggregation in sociological research." Chapel Hill: University of North Carolina.

MOORMAN, J. E. (1977) "Aggregation bias in the case of fertility differentials." M.S. thesis, University of Wisconsin.

RINDFUSS, R. (1974) "Annual fertility rates from census data: methods, assumptions, and limitations." Working Paper (74-21). Madison: University of Wisconsin Center for Demography and Ecology.

ROBINSON, G. K. (1950) "Ecological correlation and the behavior of individuals." Amer. Soc. Rev. 15: 351-357.

SCHEUCH, E. (1969) "Social context and individual behavior," pp. 133-156 in M. Dogan and S. Rokkan (eds.) Social Ecology. Cambridge: M.I.T. Press.

———— (1966) "Cross-national comparisons using aggregate data: some substantive and methodological problems," pp. 131-168 in R. Merritt and S. Rokkan (eds.) Comparing Nations. New Haven and London: Yale Univ. Press.

SCHUESSLER, K. (1969) "Covariance analysis in sociological research," pp. 219-244 in E. Borgatta (ed.) Sociological Methodology, 1969. San Francisco: Jossey-Bass.

Jeanne E. Moorman is currently a graduate student in Sociology at the University of Wisconsin-Madison. Her research is supported by a National Research Service Award Training Grant in Demography and Ecology from the National Institute for Child Health and Human Development.

HOUSEHOLD MIGRATION PLANS   8
A Multivariate Probit Model

LILLIAN M. RUSSELL
NORFLEET W. RIVES, Jr.
University of Delaware

REGRESSION WITH
BINARY DEPENDENT VARIABLES

The model of migrant behavior focusing on household migration plans has the general form:

$$Y = A + B_1X_1 + \ldots B_nX_n + E, \qquad [1]$$

where Y is the dependent variable representing planned migration, X_1 through X_n are independent variables representing

AUTHORS' NOTE: *An earlier version of this article was presented at the annual meeting of the American Statistical Association.*

demographic, economic, and social factors associated with the migration decision, A and B_1 through B_n are regression coefficients, and E is the residual term. Since planned migration is measured by the presence or absence of migration plans during a particular reference period, the dependent variable Y is binary, and the usual methods of least-squares estimation cannot be applied to equation 1. The problem arises in the following manner.

Least-squares estimation assumes that the error term E is normally distributed with zero mean and constant variance; a constant variance implies the property of homoscedasticity. The normality of residuals permits valid significance tests, while the presence of homoscedasticity permits variance estimation conditional on the independent variables. When the dependent variable is effectively continuous over the range of estimation, these two assumptions will usually be satisfied, at least to some minimal degree. When the dependent variable is binary, however, both assumptions are violated, and least-squares estimation serves no useful purpose (Palmer and Carlson, 1976; Goldberger, 1964).

PROBIT ANALYSIS

One solution to the dichotomous regressand problem is the use of probit analysis (Finney, 1971; Pindyck and Rubinfeld, 1976). The probit method can be illustrated with an example.

Suppose the index K measures the attitude of an individual toward buying an automobile. The index should be chosen so that the larger its value, the more likely the individual is to make the purchase. If income is a factor in the decision, then one can hypothesize the relation:

$$K = c_0 + c_1 I, \qquad [2]$$

where I is the level of income and c_0 and c_1 are parameters. Other variables affecting the decision independently of income might also be added to the model.

Suppose now a critical value of K can be identified for each member of some study population. Designating this value K_c, one can formulate the following decision rule. If, for each individual, the index K exceeds its critical value, then the purchase will be made. If, however, the converse is true, then the purchase will not be made.

The probit method assumes that the critical value K_c is a normally distributed random variable. The probability that K_c is less than or equal to K—the probability that an individual buys a car—can be computed from the cumulative normal distribution. Values of the index K can be obtained from the inverse of the cumulative distribution function. Since the cumulative normal transformation is nonlinear, the coefficients of equation 2 should be estimated using maximum-likelihood procedures rather than ordinary least-squares.

The probit model is one of two popular specifications of the linear probability model involving the use of cumulative probability functions. The other specification is the logit model (Pindyck and Rubinfeld, 1976). While the probit model is based on the cumulative normal distribution, the logit model is based on the cumulative logistic distribution. Since the two models are conceptually similar, it is appropriate to note their differences. First, from a purely theoretical standpoint, the logit model appears to be the stronger specification; some statisticians contend that the probit formulation is not quite as flexible. Second, from a more practical standpoint, the cost of parameter estimation may be somewhat greater with probit methods. Both models require nonlinear procedures, but the logit specification is more susceptible to linear approximations.

There is also a slight difference in the accessibility of estimation algorithms for the two models. The difference favors probit analysis, but neither model can claim routine availability of computer programs. The Statistical Package for the Social Science (SPSS), one of the most popular collections of statistical routines, does not contain options for either probit of logit estimation. Two other general-purpose packages, the Statistical Analysis System (SAS) and the Biomedical Computer Programs

(BIOMED), contain only options for univariate probit analysis. The International Mathematical and Statistical Library (IMSL), like SPSS, does not contain either probit or logit options.

The growing use of probit and logit analysis in social science research should foster the development of computer programs for parameter estimation, especially programs available on the more popular statistical packages. Until then, however, users will simply have to write their own probit and logit programs or acquire programs prepared for special purposes at other computing installations. The statistical routine used in this paper was originally developed at the University of Wisconsin and adapted for use at the University of Delaware by the Delaware Computing Center. Designated program DICHOT, the routine produces maximum-likelihood coefficient estimates and selected summary measures for probit equations containing as many as 50 independent variables. DICHOT also generates the probability associated with each case.[1]

A multivariate algorithm for probit estimation routinely available through the Delaware Computing Center strongly influenced the decision to construct a probit model of household migration plans rather than a logit model. The possibility that the two models would not produce substantially different results also influenced the decision. Nonetheless, it would be interesting to examine parameter estimates for the logit specification, comparing them with their probit counterparts. A multivariate logit procedure now being developed at the Delaware Computing Center should afford such an opportunity in the not-too-distant future.

MODELING HOUSEHOLD MIGRATION PLANS

The probit method is appropriate for building models of household migration plans because the basic information one can expect to obtain on planned migration warrants the use of a binary dependent variable. The response is coded 1 if the household plans to move from its present location during the reference period and 0 if the household does not plan to move during this period.

The parameters of a multivariate probit model of household migration plans were estimated using responses from a 1976 survey of 3,610 metropolitan Delaware households. The purpose of the survey was to produce current statistics on population and housing for local planning. Several different reference periods for the planned move were used on the survey schedule; the one selected for analysis in this paper is the six-month period. Each respondent indicated whether the household of which he or she was an immediate member had definite plans to move from its present location during the next six months. The survey design did not provide an opportunity to gauge the strength of these plans. This information would have added an interesting dimension to the analysis, not to mention the possibility of monitoring the sample households during the reference period to determine the extent to which moving plans were actually realized.

The list of subject items contained on the survey includes a series of variables one might expect to influence the propensity to move. Many of these variables have been identified on more than one occasion in the professional literature (Greenwood, 1975; Shaw, 1975; Duncan and Newman, 1976; Morrison, 1971; Navratil and Doyle, 1977; U.S. Bureau of the Census, 1978). Whether the same factors that affect observed migration also affect migration intentions remains a fundamental research question. The following variables were selected for the probit model:

MOVFRG: A binary variable equal to 1 if the household had moved at least once in the last five years, 0 otherwise.

LARES: A binary variable equal to 1 if the most recent residence of the household was in Delaware, 0 otherwise.

EDHEAD: A variable representing the education level of the head of the household. The values are:

   0 = No formal education

   1 = Elementary school (grades 1-8)

   2 = Some high school (grades 9-11)

3 = High school graduate (grade 12)
4 = Some college
5 = College graduate
6 = Postgraduate training, master's level.
7 = Postgraduate training, doctoral level

SEXHD: A binary variable equal to 1 if the head of the household is male, 0 otherwise.

MARSTA: A binary variable equal to 1 if the head of the household is married, spouse present, 0 otherwise.

RACE: A binary variable equal to 1 if the head of the household is white, 0 otherwise.

PERBED: Number of persons in the household divided by the number of bedrooms.

OWNBY: A binary variable equal to 1 if the housing unit is owned by its occupants, 0 otherwise.

CHILD: A binary variable equal to 1 if at least one person under age 19 resides in the household, 0 otherwise.

ELDER: A binary variable equal to 1 if at least one person aged 65 or over resides in the household, 0 otherwise.

RET: A binary variable equal to 1 if the head of the household is retired, 0 otherwise.

SINGLE: A binary variable equal to 1 if the household contains only one member (primary individual), 0 otherwise.

EMPL: A binary variable equal to 1 if the head of the household is currently employed, 0 otherwise. The category 1 includes both full-time and part-time work. The category 0 includes students, military personnel, and other heads who might be expected to display special (atypical) migrant behavior.

The dependent variable in the probit model if MOVPL, a binary variable equal to 1 if the household plans to move within the next six months, 0 otherwise.

The variable MOVFRG was selected for analysis because recent research indicates that persons with a history of movement have a greater propensity for subsequent migration (Da Vanzo, 1976a). The variable LARES was included in an effort to characterize the distance involved in the last move; the variable permits some distinction between interstate and intrastate migration.

The variables EDHEAD, SEXHD, MARSTA, RACE, and EMPL summarize certain demographic, economic, and social dimensions of the household, focusing on the characteristics of the head. An income variable, probably conspicuous by its absence, was present on the survey schedule, but the item did not perform well in an interview situation, and plans to include the variable in the analysis were abandoned. The variables representing characteristics of the head almost certainly capture the essence of socioeconomic status.

The variable PERBED was selected in an attempt to measure crowding within the housing unit, crowding which might prompt a search for more spacious quarters, possibly in the same general neighborhood (Rossi, 1955; Foote and others, 1960). Finally, the variables CHILD, ELDER, RET, and SINGLE were selected to represent households at what might be described as different stages of the family life cycle.

FINDINGS AND DISCUSSION

Table 1 presents parameter estimates and summary measures for the multivariate probit model of household migration plans derived from the Delaware survey. Several dimensions of the model can be evaluated.

The first dimension is the significance of regression coefficients. Since the sample size is quite large, the ratio of each coefficient to its standard error is approximately normally distributed under the null hypothesis that the true coefficient does not differ from zero. Seven of the coefficients shown in Table 1 are significant at the 5% level, while several of these are significant at higher levels. Two of the significant variables measure the extent of recent migration and the distance associated with moving, while the remaining five summarize the major characteristics of the household head.

The signs of the regression coefficients in probit analysis can be interpreted as increments or decrements to the dependent-variable probability. If a sign is positive, then this indicates that

TABLE 1
Parameter Estimates and Summary Measures:
Multivariate Probit Model of Household Migration Plans

Variable	Maximum Likelihood Coefficient Estimate	Asymtotic t-Ratio
MOVFRG	0.25	2.87
LARES	-0.22	-2.56
EDHEAD	0.04	2.16
SEXHD	0.31	2.11
MARSTA	0.33	2.19
RACE	-0.56	-2.62
PERBED	0.14	1.75
OWNBY	-0.90	-9.56
CHILD	-0.44	-0.46
ELDER	-0.36	-1.87
RET	-0.28	-1.31
SINGLE	-0.19	-1.18
EMPL	-0.22	-1.80

larger values of the variable in question (or the presence of the attribute in question for a binary independent variable) are associated with larger dependent rates of occurrence. If a sign is negative, then this indicates just the opposite. An examination of the probit coefficients shown in Table 1 produces the observation that a household is more likely to have plans to move if

- it has moved at least once in the last five years.
- the most recent move was not a local move (the last place of residence was outside Delaware),

- the household is crowded in its present quarters (the ratio of persons to bedrooms is high),
- the head of the household is well-educated,
- the head of the household is married,
- the head of the household is not white,
- the head of the household is male,
- the head of the household is not employed,
- the occupants of the household do not own their residence.

These findings conform generally to the findings of other studies of migrant behavior and the migration decision. Current research has begun to provide further evidence on the relatively greater mobility of ethnic minority households and households confronted by temporarily adverse economic conditions (U.S. Bureau of the Census, 1978).

The life cycle variables, CHILD, ELDER, RET, and SINGLE, do not appear to have a common effect on moving plans. Only the variable ELDER is statistically significant at even the 10% level. According to the negative sign of the coefficients, a household is less likely to plan to move if

- it contains at least one child under age 19,
- it contains at least one person aged 65 or over,
- the head of the household is retired,
- the head of the household is the only household member.

The first three findings do not contradict what is known generally about the factors inhibiting mobility. The fourth finding is somewhat surprising, however. Students of migration have traditionally considered single-person households more mobile. A probable explanation is that the negative sign of the coefficient of the variable SINGLE is correct and the traditional pattern of primary-individual mobility is simply not applicable to metropolitan Delaware households. Changing attitudes toward marriage and family formation, combined with the growing incidence of divorce, have almost certainly begun to alter the demographic, economic, and social structure of single-person households in some areas of the United States, possibly reducing their mobility relative to other groups (Kobrin, 1976). National surveys continue to indicate, however, that primary individuals move at greater rates than larger households, although more recent estimates of the difference are quite small (U.S. Bureau of the Census, 1975, 1978).

The second dimension of the model that should be evaluated is goodness-of-fit. The usual approach to goodness-of-fit is the computation of the coefficient of multiple determination (R^2), but the concept of R^2 as a measure of goodness-of-fit loses some of its meaning when the dependent variable is binary. Several studies have shown that the upper limit of R^2 for linear models with dichotomous dependent variables may be substantially less than one (Neter and Maynes, 1970; Morrison, 1972). The prospect of no unique upper limit confounds the interpretation of the probit R^2, diluting its usefulness for the purpose of model evaluation. Program DICHOT, the probit estimation algorithm used in this paper, does not contain an option for the computation of R^2. Consequently, no estimate of R^2 is available for the model shown in Table 1.

Program DICHOT does provide an estimate of the test statistic for the log-likelihood ratio test. The purpose of the test is to determine whether the model with the explanatory variables is significantly better than the model incorporating only a constant term. The test is conceptually similar to the F-test of least-squares regression. The log-likelihood ratio test statistic is computed from the generalized likelihood ratio test statistic, the ratio of the maximum of the likelihood function for the model with only a constant term (no explanatory variables) to the maximum of the likelihood function for the model with the full variable complement. The logarithm of this ratio, the log-likelihood ratio test statistic, is a measure of the difference between the two models, or, more precisely, the relative contribution of the explanatory variables. When the log-likelihood ratio is multiplied by –2, the ratio has an asymptotic chi-square distribution with the number of degrees of freedom equal to the number of independent variables in the probit model. The log-likelihood ratio for the model shown in Table 1 is 284.4 with 13 degrees of freedom. The probability of a larger value in the appropriate chi-square distribution is less than 0.001. This is sufficient to demonstrate that the model with the explanatory variables is significantly better than the model incorporating only a constant term.

Whether an even better model can be found, possibly one containing fewer variables or one involving different variables, cannot be determined solely on the basis of the log-likelihood ratio test. This test permits only a comparison of two models with and without a given set of independent variables. It can indicate whether variable set A is better than just the constant term, but not whether variable set A is better than variable set B. A more rigorous evaluation of alternative probit specifications must await further refinements in the measurement of goodness-of-fit.

AGGREGATE PROBIT ESTIMATION

The probability model developed in this paper has applications at several levels of aggregation. The most obvious level is the individual household, where the model can be used to generate probability estimates for households with different characteristic profiles. The most potentially useful level, however, at least from the standpoint of planning and policy analysis, is the community. Consider the following situation.

Suppose local planners are interested in the impact of migration on the fiscal stability of their community and would like to develop a technique that would permit them to predict household moves several time periods into the future. The model presented in this paper, with its emphasis on the relaiton of current household characteristics to anticipated migration over the next six months, could serve this purpose. But one modification would have to be made before the model could be applied at the community level.

When the probit model is used to compute the probability that a household with a given characteristic profile will plan to move during the reference period, the values of the independent variables correspond to the profile of the household in question. Thus, for example, the sex of the head is either male or female, and the household either has or has not moved at least once in the last five years. When the probit model is extended to higher levels of aggregation, the same coding scheme cannot be employed. The binomial variables representing household attributes must be replaced by proportions, and the measured variables must be replaced by means and medians. Thus, for example, the binary variable representing a primary individual would be replaced by the proportion of households in the community containing only one person. And the measured variable representing household crowding would be replaced by the average number of persons per bedroom.

Extending the probit model to the community level would enable planners to generate probabilities of planning to move for the entire population of community households. The probabilities should be interpreted as proportions planning to move, and they can be applied to current demographic estimates to determine the probable extent of household migration for the immediate future. There can be no question that information of this type is potentially useful in a wide range of planning and policy applications, but it is important to note that the model will yield estimates only for the household population at a given point in time. This means that the model is limited to the moving plans of area residents, regardless of their anticipated destination. Migration into the community by residents of other areas would not be covered under this scheme.

Values of the independent variables for the community-level version of the probit model can be census figures, postcensal estimates, or information drawn from local administrative-record systems. Most of the independent variables shown in Table 1 have empirical counterparts in one of these areas. When the ultimate purpose of a probit model is to produce aggregate probability estimates, special consideration should be given to the correspondence between micro-level variables used for model construction and possible macro-level counterparts.

The utility of an aggregate probit model can be substantially increased by the prospect of its application in situations different from that associated with parameter estimation. The utility of the community-level migration model, for example, a model derived from a 1976 metropolitan Delaware survey, could be increased if the model were found to be useful when applied to (1) the same geographic area in a different year, (2) a different area in the same year, or (3) a different area in a different year. There is no guarantee, of course, that any of these alternative applications will prove successful, and each one should be approached with some degree of caution. Different areas at the same point in time may not exhibit the same pattern of planned migration, even though they appear to be demographically, economically, and socially similar. Furthermore, the same area at different points in time may exhibit structural relations between planned migration and its ecological covariates that cannot be adequately described by a single model. Generally, however, one can expect areas with similar demographic, economic, and social characteristics to exhibit similar patterns of planned migration.

The utility of aggregate probit estimation can also be substantially increased by the prospect of using models constructed at one level of aggregation to produce probability estimates for component areas at a lower level. Thus, for example, a probit model derived from a statewide survey might be used to generate probability estimates for areas within the state, such as cities, counties, or minor civil divisions. The central issue raised in the preceding paragraph is the major issue surrounding the use of an increasingly popular technique called synthetic estimation (Mooney and Rives, 1978). If counties, for example, were homogeneous with respect to planned migration and its covariates, then a probit model constructed from a statewide survey could be profitably applied at the county level. A probit model developed from survey responses at one level of aggregation and used to produce probability estimates at lower levels represents an efficient use of the survey information, but there is always the possibility that the component areas in question are ecologically quite different, at least with respect to variables of interest. Applications of the probit method beyond the circumstances surrounding model construction should always be approached with some degree of caution.

NOTE

1. Persons interested in obtaining a copy of the technical documentation for the program should address their inquiries to the Delaware Computing Center, University of Delaware, Newark, Delaware 19711.

REFERENCES

Da VANZO, J. (1976a) "Differences between return and nonreturn migration: an econometric analysis." Int. Migration Rev. 10: 13-27.

——— (1976b) Why Families Move: A Model of the Geographic Mobility of Married Couples. Report No. R-1972-DOL. Santa Monica: Rand.

DUNCAN, G. and S. NEWMAN (1976) "Expected and actual residential mobility." J. of the Amer. Institute of Planners 42: 174-186.

FINNEY, D. (1971) Probit Analysis. New York: Cambridge Univ. Press.

FOOTE, N. et al. (1960) Housing Choices and Housing Constraints. New York: McGraw-Hill.

GOLDBERGER, A. (1964) Econometric Theory. New York: John Wiley.

GREENWOOD, M. (1975) "Research on internal migration in the United States: a survey." J. of Economic Literature 13: 397-433.

KOBRIN, F. (1976) "The fall in household size and the rise of the primary individual in the United States." Demography 13: 127-138.

MOONEY, A. and N. RIVES (1978) "Measures of community health status for health planning." Health Services Research 13 (summer): 129-145.

MORRISON, D. G. (1972) "Upper bounds for correlations between binary outcomes and probabilistic predictions." J. of the Amer. Statistical Assn. 67: 68-70.

MORRISON, P. A. (1971) The Propensity to Move: A Longitudinal Analysis. Report No. R-654-HUD. Santa Monica: Rand.

NAVRATIL, F. and J. DOYLE (1977) "The socioeconomic determinants of migration and the level of aggregation." Southern Economic Journal 43: 1547-1559.

NETER, J. and E. MAYNES (1970) "Correlation coefficient with a (0, 1) dependent variable." J. of the Amer. Statistical Assn. 65: 501-509.

PALMER, J. and P. CARLSON (1976) "Problems with the use of regression analysis in prediction studies." J. of Research in Crime and Delinquency 13: 64-81.

PINDYCK, R. and D. RUBINFELD (1976) Econometric Models and Economic Forecasts. New York: McGraw-Hill.

ROSSI, P. (1955) Why Families Move. New York: Free Press.

SHAW, R. (1975) Migration Theory and Fact. Bibliography Series No. 5. Regional Science Research Institute.

SHRYOCK, H. and J. SIEGEL (1976) The Methods and Materials of Demography. Condensed Edition by E. Stockwell. New York: Academic Press.

U.S. Bureau for the Census (1975) "Mobility of the population of the United States: March 1970 to March 1975." Current Population Reports, Series P-20, No. 285. Washington, DC: U.S. Government Printing Office.

U.S. Bureau of the Census (1978) "Geographical mobility: March 1975 to March 1977." Current Population Reports, Series P-20, No. 320. Washington, DC: U.S. Government Printing Office.

Lillian M. Russell is a doctoral candidate in the College of Urban Affairs and Public Policy at the University of Delaware. Her major interest is the application of quantitative methods to the study of social change.

Norfleet W. Rives, Jr. is Associate Professor in the College of Urban Affairs and Public Policy and the Department of Mathematical Sciences at the University of Delaware. His major interest is the role of population estimates and projections in planning and public policy.

DAVID J. JACKSON
National Institute of Mental Health
EDGAR F. BORGATTA
City University of New York
HAROLD F. GOLDSMITH
National Institute of Mental Health

*f*actorial ecology may be defined as the investigation of residential differentiation of subunits of urban areas, e.g., census tracts, by means of common factor analysis or related procedures. This research endeavor raises many interesting but difficult conceptual and methodological issues. The interpretation and design of factorial ecology research will be advanced by the formulation of explicit and systematic statements of data analysis strategies. In the following discussion, one approach to this task is outlined. The discussion is organized around a data analysis question which has been discussed in the factorial ecology literature (Hunter, 1972): "What are the relative merits of common factor analysis and component analysis procedures for factorial ecology research?" Any reasonable answer to this question presupposes a set of criteria by which one assesses these alternative data analysis procedures. The research strategy outlined here provides criteria for answering this question.

THREE BASIC QUESTIONS

In preparing an answer to the question of the relative merits of common factor and component procedures, three important questions must be considered: (1) What are the conceptual differences and similarities between these alternative methods of analysis? (2) What are the research objectives of factorial ecology? (3) What are the special properties of census tract data, if any, which need to be considered in the selection of a data analysis procedure? Other criteria may also be useful in the selection of a data analysis procedure. However, these three questions are of primary importance.

A RESEARCH OBJECTIVE
FOR FACTORIAL ECOLOGY

"Parsimonious data reduction" and/or the discovery of "fundamental dimensions of residential differentiation" have been proposed as the objectives of factorial ecology. For various reasons these two objectives are of limited usefulness. The following objective is consistent with these two objectives, but of prior and more fundamental importance. The objective is to discover sets of observed variables that display a *nontrivial* pattern of association (structure) across different cities and for the same city at different points in time. In short, the primary task is to discover empirically stable regularities. After the existence of stable, nontrivial patterns of covariation for particular sets of variables under specified conditions has been established, we will have a firm foundation for substantive-theoretical interpretation of these empirically stable patterns.

Before turning to a brief consideration of some relevant properties of census tract data, it is appropriate to note a few observations on the significance of stable covariance structures. While there is little hesitation in endorsing the scientific importance of establishing the existence of stable structures, the significance of such structures, if they exist, is not a simple issue. They may arise in a number of different ways, and the source of the covariation determines the importance that can be attributed to them.

(1) Trivially Redundant Content. A set of measures with a stable structure may be empirically and theoretically trivial if the

covariation is due to artifactual dependencies among the measures. For example, a set of five alternative measures of fertility which share very similar parts in their operational definition may have a stable covariance structure. However, this stability would to some extent be a trivial consequence of the shared parts, not a reflection of some empirical unity of covariation. Some sets of measures used in factorial ecology research are of this type.

(2) Common Causal Antecedents. A stable covariance structure may be in part due to the measures having a common causal antecedent (or set of highly correlated common causal antecedents).

(3) Developmental Unity. Growth processes may be expressed in terms of stable covariance structures under certain conditions. For example, a set of anatomical and physiological measures on a class of organisms at different stages of maturation may form a stable covariance structure. The consistently high and positive correlations between such measures as height, body weight, and length of forearms may be represented as a size factor, or under other circumstances may be simply an age factor. The pattern is due to a common developmental process, and not to some latent causal variable such as size. The size of an organism does not cause body weight or height; a unity of body weight, height, and other such measures is what is usually named "size."

(4) Causal Dependence Between Variables. A set of variables which are causally interrelated would, under some circumstances, display a stable covariance structure. For example, the stable associations between some housing characteristics and some household characteristics are to some extent undoubtedly due to causal dependence between these variables. If the type of housing in an area is changed in a particular manner, a change in the characteristics of the households that take up residence in this area may result.

(5) Unimagined Processes That Generate Stable Covariance Structures. In the early part of this century, Spearman's general

factor theory of human abilities seemed to be a compelling causal explanation of the stable patterns of covariance in ability measures. The g-factor as a latent causal variable seemed to be the only possible alternative. However, Godfrey Thomson (1919 and 1939) was able to construct a "bond" sampling process model of the functioning of the brain which could also account for the observed stable covariance structures (Maxwell, 1977). It is of interest to note that Thomson's theory would in all likelihood not have been developed in the absence of Spearman's causal model which called attention to an important general empirical pattern. We should be open to the possibility that some presently unknown model of urban change can account for the stable patterns of covariation among census tract variables. The systematic demonstration of the existence of these assumed stable covariance structures may make an important contribution to the development of such a model.

If, under specified conditions, there are stable patterns of covariation for certain sets of census variables, they may be due to combinations of the above possibilities. At the present time we have no sound a priori grounds for explaining stable patterns of covariation between census tract variables. The stable patterns which are currently thought to be present in census tract data may be due, to a significant extent, to trivial and artifactual reasons.

We now turn to a brief consideration of a few relevant properties of census tract data.

SPECIAL PROPERTIES OF CENSUS TRACT DATA RELEVANT TO FACTORIAL ECOLOGY

Any property of census tract data which is apt to have a systematic and predictable effect on the results of a component or common factor analysis is a relevant property. As an example of a relevant data property, consider an example from another area of research. Much of the literature on component and factor analysis is developed within the context of continuous measures and multivariate normal distribution theory. Psychologists were quick to realize that when these methods were extended to data which poorly approximated these assumptions, special allowances needed to be made. One of the important properties of normally distributed variables is that the means and variances of these variables are independent. However, if one is analyzing dichotomous variables—i.e., the only admissible scores are zero or unity—a metric problem arises. In this case, there is a dependency between the means and variances of the measures. When phi-coefficients are analyzed using common factor analysis, or principal component analysis, "spurious" factors (components) may emerge. These factors (components) will have loadings roughly proportional to the means of dichotomous variables (Lawley, 1944; Maxwell, 1977). If one desires, analytic procedures may be used to remove such factors (components) from the correlation matrix prior to the analysis. Additional problems are discussed in the psychological literature on factor analysis, e.g., method factors, response sets, and ipsative items. Similar issues need to be addressed by factorial ecologists in their investigation of census tract data. While there is a rudimentary awareness of these issues, as evidenced by the occasional use of (nonlinear) transformations of certain variables prior to an analysis, their importance needs to be highlighted and sytematically explored. We now call attention to a few of these properties of census tract data.

(a) Census Tracts as Samples. In most factorial ecology studies, there is no apparent sense in which the data under analysis is a sample. There are some instances in which the tracts under analysis do form a sample from a larger universe of census tracts (Borgatta and Hadden, 1977); however, in most cases, the investigator has data on all the tracts of interest. One might consider conceptualizing all the tracts for a particular metropolitan area as a sample of alternative area units. At best, tracts have only an approximate conceptual meaning in terms of the guidelines the Census Bureau recommends to local tract committees. An actual set of tracts might be viewed as a sample from the set of boundaries that alternative tract committees might have generated. It is

of some importance to know the extent to which factorial ecology results are contingent upon the definition of area units. This is an avenue of investigation which has been explored to some extent.

(b) Unreliability of Tract Variables. Response error is undoubtedly present at the individual household and enumerator level of data collection. Missing data due to suppression may be represented to some degree in terms of unreliability. While the Census Bureau strives to maintain high standards of reliability, its procedures are not designed to maximize reliability for the somewhat nebulous interests of factorial ecology. For example, the weighting of some item counts may also have unanticipated effects on the reliability of tract measures. This question of reliability is related to the communality estimates reported in factorial ecology investigations. It is not unusual to find some measures with communalities approaching unity for correlation matrices. Are the data really this reliable, or are there other neglected properties of tract data that account for these questionably large communalities? At this time, we only wish to indicate that this is an issue requiring consideration.

(c) Complex Variables. Most of the variables constructed to represent household and housing unit properties of census tracts are complex variables. The typical factorial ecology variable is a rate with respect to some subpopulation of the tract; for example, low occupation status (males) is the number of males employed in low-status occupations divided by the total number of employed males. This is a ratio of the size of one subpopulation to the size of another subpopulation of a tract. Sets of variables may be ratios with identical or very similar denominators, e.g., youth dependency ratio and elderly dependency ratio. An examination of the scatter diagram of pairs of these variables will often show a striking departure from linear association. These types of data raise serious data analysis and interpretation problems. They may lead to "factors" that reflect the analytic structure of the data (such as the dichotomous variable example at the beginning of this section) or to "factors" that reflect nonlinear aspects

of the association between variables. We actually know very little about the analysis and interpretation problems due to these complexities. While there is a literature related to the analysis of rate variables, it has not been systematically related to the methods and objectives of factorial ecology.

(d) Undefined Tract Variables. It is possible to construct census tract variables which are undefined for some tracts, or have only an arbitrary definition. Any variable which has some subpopulation as a base is not defined for any tract for which this subpopulation is absent. For example, medium rent of Negro-occupied units is not defined for tracts that are 100% non-Negro. Percent families in poverty is not defined for tracts that have no family households. This raises the question of just what variables and types of tracts are appropriate for a factorial ecology investigation.

SELECTING A DATA ANALYSIS METHOD
FOR FACTORIAL ECOLOGY

We now return to our initial question: "Is common factor, principal components, or image analysis more appropriate for factorial ecology?" If we recall that the assumed objective of factorial ecology is the discovery of stable covariance structures across cities and time, none of these methods in terms of their *standard* conceptualization would appear technically to be appropriate for factorial ecology.

Common factor analysis is conceptualized in terms of *assumed latent variables.* Incomplete standardized principal components and rescaled image analysis are typically presented as approximations of common factor analysis, which supposedly avoids some problems associated with the common factor model—the number of factors (communality estimation) and indeterminant factor scores. These advantages are more apparent than real. For example, Kaiser (1963) argues that k (the number of eigenvalues of the rescaled image covariance matrix greater than unity) should be retained for rotation and interpretation. He presents four different arguments for this recommendation (Kaiser, 1963). Each argument presupposes that the common factor model is true. If we reject the common factor model's latent variable conceptualization, there are no grounds for employing any of these procedures unless some appropriate alternative interpretation is offered.

Any covariance matrix of more than a few variables presents a major challenge to a researcher attempting to identify potentially important patterns of association. This challenge is greatly magnified when the task requires one to establish that there are similar patterns of association present in multiple covariance matrices. Consequently, it is no surprise that factorial ecologists have adopted methods such as common factor or component analysis for analyzing covariance matrices. These methods may be effectively employed *without* any appeal to latent variables or fundamental variables that supposedly account for observed covariance. *The major contribution of these procedures is that they facilitate the recognition of patterns of association that may not be easy to detect or describe in a raw covariance matrix.* These procedures are analogous to mathematical notation. Many mathematical relations that would be extremely complex to represent and difficult to demonstrate using scalar algebra notation become rather simple when matrix notation and manipulation rules are employed. Definite patterns of association that might not be recognized in a covariance matrix may become obvious when appropriate transformations are applied to the covariance matrices.

If trivially small differences between the matrices of covariances for a set of variables for two cities are found, this would begin to provide "evidence" that there was a stable covariance structure for these variables. However, if we find that there are striking differences between the covariance matrices, this would not per se discount the hypothesis that there is some unrecognized stable pattern(s) present. A transformation of the covariance matrices to correlation matrices might be sufficient to disclose the stable pattern(s). This simple metric transformation may also prove to be inadequate for accenting stable patterns of association across cities. Failure to find evidence for stable covariance structures at the covariance or the correlation level by using simple subtraction procedures might suggest the use of principal component analysis to define reference axes for representing the covariance structures in order to describe patterns of association stable across cities. If

$$\Sigma = P \triangle P'$$

is a principal component type decomposition of Σ,

$$C = (\text{diag } \Sigma)^{-1/2} P \triangle^{1/2}$$

could be interpreted as a matrix of correlations between the observed variables and the P orthogonal reference axes. A failure to find similar C matrices based on the observed covariance matrix for two different cities might lead to a consideration of a similar analysis based on the observed correlation matrices. Notice that in this analysis principal component type procedures are used to define orthogonal reference axes which may disclose stable patterns of covariation. We need make no appeal to the principal components of the observed variables as some sort of fundamental variables. However, in later stages of the development of factorial ecology, we may wish to calculate components based on this type of analysis.

Attention is also called to the fact that we have not used any arbitrary rule for discarding those reference axes associated with principal components with small variances. If the purpose were to construct a relatively small set of composites to approximate the information in the initial set of P variables, some sort of cutoff rule would be useful. However, this is not our present purpose. If we were to find stable patterns across cities for reference axes associated with small eigenvalues, would we want to ignore them just because the variance of the associated component is small? Probably not. However, it would be a welcomed reduction in complexity if one did have some justification for reducing the dimensionality of the observed covariance matrix.

With respect to the declared purpose, the reference axes associated with the principal components definition is rather arbitrary. It may or may not lead to the recognition of similar patterns of association. Any rotation, orthogonal or oblique, which leads to the recognition of patterns of association which are stable across cities would be appropriate. "Simple structure" criteria as expressed in quartimax, varimax, or promax rotation procedures could be employed. Their use need not be based on any belief that these rotations lead to substantively important structures that indicate the presence of "fundamental" latent variables. If a set of variables is composed of subsets of variables which highly correlate within a subset and have a smaller degree of association with variables in other subsets, rotation procedures may aid in the recognition and description of such patterns. Blind faith, however, should not be placed in these mechanical procedures to point out stable patterns of covariation automatically.

While the analysis suggested in the last few paragraphs is reasonably appropriate for the objective of factorial ecology, it does have a number of undesirable properties. These procedures are dependent upon the scaling of the observed variables. This is an especially serious limitation when the major objective is the comparison of structures across different cities for which the variances may be radically different. Another drawback is that the above analysis of p variables requires the examination of p reference axes. It would be desirable to have a rank reduction and "scale-free" procedure consistent with the research objectives and the known properties of census tract data. This suggests a reconsideration of image analysis or common factor analysis since both are in a sense "scale-free" and rank reduction procedures. Since rescaled image analysis as presented by Harris and Kaiser is inherently an approximation to common factor analysis, an independent justification of this procedure for our purposes would be required, or an appropriate rationale for common factor analysis.

Consider the following representation of y, a (p x 1) vector of centered observed variables,

$$y = c + s + r.$$

The (p $\times$ 1) vector, r, represents the aggregation of all sources of random disturbances on the elements of y. When the number of census tracts is sufficiently large, it would not be unreasonable to consider the elements of r to be uncorrelated and approximately normally distributed. This interpretation would not be appropriate if Σ, the (p $\times$ p) covariance matrix, were not positive definite.

The (p $\times$ 1) vector s represents a part of y which contributes to the variance of observed variables, but not the covariance of observed variables. The remaining part, c, is a (p $\times$ 1) vector of common parts, i.e., parts of observed variables which covary. The s and r vectors are, by definition, uncorrelated with each other and the vector of common parts. In the following discussion we will combine s and r as a residual vector. While the distinction between the specific and error parts will have no consequences for the following development, the concept of a vector of specific parts is useful for accounting for some observed phenomena. This representation leads to the following covariance structure of Σ.

$$\Sigma = \Omega + \Psi$$

Ψ is a diagonal matrix of residual covariances while Ω is a matrix of the covariance of common parts. The residual covariance matrix, Ψ, is of rank p by definition. The rank of Ω is k. The technical literature on factor analysis enables us to state that

$$\alpha < k$$

where α is Guttman's "best" lower bound on the number of common factors (the number of positive eigenvalues of R - S, where s = $[\text{diag } \Sigma^{-1}]^{-1}$). Maximum likelihood procedures would be optimal for estimating Ψ for given values of k. These procedures, as Brown (1967) and Howe (1955) have demonstrated, may be justified apart from any distribution assumptions. If k is permitted to be sufficiently large, a Ψ can always be found which makes Ω of rank k. Since our primary interest is to find a minimum number of reference axes for representing the covariance structure of our observed variables which is consistent with our provision for unique and random error variance in the observed variables, the minimum k consistent with Σ - Ω being a good approximation of a diagonal matrix will satisfy our purposes. The maximum likelihood definition of Λ, where $\Omega = \Lambda \Lambda'$, would be used to define the correlations between the p observed variables and the k reference axes. Simple structure rotations, orthogonal or oblique, could be used to help identify patterns of covariation.

The major advantages of using maximum likelihood procedures for defining Λ and Ψ relative to a rescaled image analysis or an incomplete standardized principal component analysis would be that these ML common factor analysis procedures assure us that Σ - Ω will be optimally close to a diagonal matrix for a given value of k. In any event, Σ - Ω should be examined for residual patterns of association when any of these three methods are used to define Λ.

While we are inclined to recommend the use of ML common factor analysis procedures for defining reference axes, any of these procedures could be effectively used. Any one of them which contributes to the establishment of evidence that a particular pattern of covariation is stable across cities and time would further the objectives of factorial ecology. The crucial issue is not to locate "factors" which are common across different methods of "factor analysis" as has been argued (Hunter, 1972), but to establish the presence of stable patterns of covariation across cities and time.

REFERENCES

BORGATTA, E. F. and J. K. HADDEN (1977) "The analysis of social areas: a critical review and some empirical data," pp. 81-144 in J. V. Ferreira and S. S. Jha (eds.) THE OUTLOOK TOWER. Bombay: Populare Prakashan.

BROWNE, M. W. (1967) Fitting the Factor Analysis Model. Research Bulletin 67-2. Princeton, NJ: Educational Testing Service.

HOWE, H. B. (1955) Some Contributions to Factor Analysis. Report No. ORNL-1919. Oak Ridge, TN: Oak Ridge National Laboratory.

HUNTER, A. A. (1972) "Factorial ecology: a critique and some suggestions." DEMOGRAPHY 9: 107-118.

KAISER, H. F. (1963) "Image analysis," in C. W. Harris (ed.) PROBLEMS IN MEASURING CHANGE. Madison: University of Wisconsin Press.

LAWLEY, D. N. (1944) "The factor analysis of multiple item tests." PROCEEDINGS OF THE ROYAL SOCIETY OF EDINBURGH. 62: 74-82.

MAXWELL, A. E. (1977) MULTIVARIATE ANALYSIS IN BEHAVIORAL RESEARCH. New York: Halsted Press.

THOMSON, G. H. (1939) The Factorial Analysis of Human Ability. Boston: Houghton Mifflin.

——— (1919) "On the cause of hierarchical order among correlation coefficients." PROCEEDINGS OF THE ROYAL SOCIETY 95: 400-408.

David J. Jackson is a research sociologist for the Population Research Section of the Mental Health Study Center, National Institute of Mental Health.

Edgar F. Borgatta is at the City University of New York Graduate Center.

Harold F. Goldsmith is Associate Chief of the Mental Health Study Center, National Institute of Mental Health.
10.71

ON DETERMINING CRITICAL HEALTH PROBLEM AREAS
New York City

10

EDGAR F. BORGATTA
MARIE L. BORGATTA
City University of New York

*i*n a recent report, Israel and Roosma (1976) present a factor analysis of health areas in Manhattan and suggest a "proxy" variable to identify relative health needs in the areas. The proxy variable "percent of population aged 5 or less who are living in female headed households" suggests such images as the ADC family unit, the deprived, and people living on the fringes of an upwardly mobile achieving society. The variables most closely associated with the proxy variable support this type of image, with the foremost being percent Black population, low median family income, little or no prenatal care, and adults having less than an eighth-grade education. It may well be that use of such a proxy variable permits understanding of an important way in which the population is distributed among the health areas, but more can be said from a closer inspection of the data.

Israel and Roosma provide a brief but useful review of concern with health indicators, focusing particularly on the orientation towards finding a single index, such as the Federal Government's Index of Medical Underservice. Their presentation notes some criticisms of indices, but skirts one basic criticism which can be stated simply.

Is a single index an appropriate way of describing the areas with regard to stated objectives of locating areas of "need" or "underservice"? The analysis and presentation that follow build on their work and extend it.

Israel and Roosma note that they used a varimax rotation and found a similar structure to the factors reported. Additional rotations are possible, and these lead to other interpretations and possible suggestions for further research. Here attention is given first to a reanalysis of the data by a purposive factor rotation, and then the use of variables is discussed.

Among the variables included in the study, some were classed as indicators of social economic status. These variables do not represent a full array of social economic variables, but in the analysis they form an identifiable cluster pivoting on "Median Family Income" and "Percent of population aged 25+ with less than 8th grade education." Other variables are highly correlated to these core variables, but usually these are not thought of as defining the concept. Thus, the association of high fertility with low social economic status is a common expectation from the research literature, as is the association to such other variables as minority group status and infant mortality. What this suggests, however, is that it might be appropriate to examine the data by rotating the factors so most of the variance of social economic status is located in one factor, and then adjusting the other factors to facilitate interpretation.

The purposive factor rotation has been carried out using the published factor loadings, and the newly rotated matrix is presented as Table 1. It should be noted that the location of the axes could have been adjusted a degree to get an exact fit, say, through the variable of Median Family Income; but since the points to be illuminated are easily read here and the computations were done by hand, the locations are approximate.

Having carried out the rotation, it is now possible to reinterpret the data. A first important statement that is possible is that Factor I' (social economic status) with Median Family Income as the pivotally defining variable involves much of the variance of the mortality and morbidity variables. Also, it happens that

TABLE 1
Published Factor Loadings Compared to Rerotated
Factor Loadings

	Published Factor Loadings				Rerotated Factor Loadings			
Socio-Economic	P_1	P_2	P_3	h^2	I'	II'	III'	h^2
Black	.77	-.08	-.22	.65	.65	.47	-.03	.64
P.R.	.32	.68	.11	.58	.54	-.41	-.35	.57
Median Family Income (-)	.90	.32	.16	.94	.97	.00	-.01	.94
Educ. < 8	.69	.30	.33	.68	.80	-.18	.09	.68
Fertility	.76	.34	.19	.73	.85	-.08	-.02	.73
Child < 6 in Fem. H. HH	.93	.04	-.17	.90	.85	.41	-.06	.89
1 Per. HH (-)	.55	.56	.31	.71	.75	-.38	-.10	.72
Overcrowded Housing	.60	-.07	.41	.53	.61	-.02	.40	.53
Mortality								
Under 7 days	.50	-.32	-.51	.61	.27	.73	-.10	.62
Male under 1 year	.59	-.37	-.29	.57	.41	.63	.09	.57
Pneumonia & Influenza	.16	-.40	.01	.19	.02	.31	.30	.19
TB	.58	-.13	.05	.36	.51	.25	.18	.36
Cirrhosis	.65	-.48	-.08	.66	.44	.59	.34	.66
Hypertension 25+	.20	-.53	.73	.85	.14	-.07	.91	.85
Female Ca.	-.30	-.64	.17	.53	-.46	.20	.53	.52
Male Ca.	-.08	-.73	.10	.55	-.29	.38	.56	.54
Digest. Ca. 45+	.10	-.57	.71	.84	.03	-.07	.91	.83
Morbidity								
TB	.59	-.34	.01	.46	.44	.42	.30	.46
Hepatitis	.55	.04	-.21	.35	.49	.31	-.12	.35
Gonorrhea	.68	-.50	-.29	.80	.42	.76	.20	.79
Resources								
MD in Priv. Practice (-)	.38	.21	.08	.20	.44	-.06	-.05	.20
Acute Beds (-)	.19	.03	.17	.07	.22	-.07	.12	.07
Utilization								
Late or no Prenatal care	.76	-.08	-.03	.59	.69	.34	.11	.60

most of the variance of Israel and Roosma's suggested proxy variable is associated with this factor.

Even more important than the simple reading of the loadings in the social economic factor, however, is the inspection of the two other factors. First of all, Factor III' can be seen to absorb the variables of "Deaths from hypertension of persons aged 25+ per 100 population aged 25+" and "Deaths from digestive cancer among persons aged 45+ per 100 population aged 45+." These variables are *rate data*; but since key age variables are not included in the study, there is no way of knowing from the array of variables whether the higher rates are due to age distribution in the area. Israel and Roosma indicate "that most of the variables were not controlled for the age distribution of the population." Here we refer to the omission of age indicators of the population itself, such as the percentage of persons 65 years of age and over. Since circulatory diseases and cancers are often thought of as degenerative diseases (as compared with communicable diseases), the factor may be associated with age characteristics of the population at least in part. A variable indicating the proportion of older persons in the health areas could provide a basis for examining this possible explanation.

Additional variables heavily loaded in this Factor III′ include the male and female cancer death rates, which again may be though of as degenerative diseases. Further examination of the loadings in this factor are suggestive of other characteristics of health. The negative loading of the "Percent of population which is Puerto Rican" is not directly explainable, but might be accounted for if Puerto Ricans are not present in communities that have older populations. Information on migration patterns suggests that older persons return to Puerto Rico.

Possibly most interesting is Factor II′, which involves variables that may be viewed as indicators of health status. This factor appears to be defined by variables that are not heavily involved in the Factor III′ indicators. Factor II′ is not defined by any of its major variables totally independently of Factor I′, and thus the loadings are necessarily lower for the defining variables of Factor II′. The defining variables are the infant mortality variables and the gonorrhea rate, rates that may be seen as potentially responsive to intervention by the health and other support services in society. These variables may be associated with forms of disorganization that are independent of poverty to at least some extent, possibly having to do with health habits and other aspects of life style. The suggestion of a contributing life style and health habits can be drawn from the types of diseases that occur in this set of loadings, such as the gonnorhea rate and the cirrhosis mortality rate. Health habits may be suggested in part by the loading on late or no prenatal care, defined here independently of income level. Life style factors are also suggested by a variable like children under 6 in female headed households. The variable of percentage Black is positively loaded in this factor in contrast to the percentage Puerto Rican, which is negatively loaded in this factor. Death and morbidity rates associated with communicable diseases are also associated with this factor. What is most important, however, is that the "Ratio of physicians in private practice in health area to population" is *not* involved in this factor, but is involved virtually only with Factor I' (social economic factor).

What is suggested from this analysis, thus, is that one way health areas may be classed in terms of medical health care needs is by social-economic variables. It is simple to rationalize that for any number of reasons the poor need more support services provided. Rationales range from not being able to afford health care to not being sufficiently educated about such matters to other selective factors such as the reluctance of doctors to practice in poor areas. But, aside from this, areas may have indicators of poor health independently of the social-economic characteristics. *Such areas thus must be identified quite separately from a classification using social-economic variables.* To identify the additional concomitants of such areas requires more information than is available in the paper here reexamined. A social concomitant to such areas in the factor analysis re-rotation is the "Percent of population which is Black." With appropriately selected variables in further analysis of these types of data, it may be possible to delineate more accurately the social concomitants of these health care indicators.

DISCUSSION AND CONCLUSION

Israel and Roosma call attention to the progress in and the problems with methods of assessing the health needs of small areas within densely populated metropolitan communities, in particular the pinpointing of areas with greatest need for primary care physicians. In evaluating need, they note the difficulty of separating the availability of resources, the use of resources, and the actual health status of the residents. (Health status is often a troublesome variable to measure because there are both objective and evaluative aspects to health status; i.e., there may be perceived need on the part of the consumer which may not meet some objective criteria of need, such as an assessment by medical personnel on the basis of symptoms.) They point out that socio-demographic variables are frequently the best predictors of level of health and community organization.

The Index of Medical Underservice (IMU) in widespread use at this time is, as the authors indicate, a weighted summary measure of 4 variables, the values of which are easily obtainable from record statistics used to evaluate the health needs of communities. The IMU has been criticized (Wysong, 1975; Kleinman and Wilson, 1977) for (a) failing to differentiate conceptually between availability of services, their use, health status, and socio-economic variables and (b) having been constructed through a system of "expert" evaluation rather than on the basis of empirical measures. In any event, even the developers of the IMU concede that it is probably not appropriate for use in densely populated areas (Health Services Research Group, 1975).

In our additional examination of the factor analysis by Israel and Roosma, we have done hand rotations of the data, and the purposive rotations are sufficiently clear to make our point. What is quickly surmised from the analysis by Israel and Roosma and the reanalysis presented here is that further useful development of the approach hinges on addition of variables to permit more refined partitioning of the sources of variance of the health indicators. The current data serve as an important basis from which more detailed studies can be formulated adding information from applied theory in the area of the delivery of health services but within the context of the current findings. It also leads to speculation on how variables need to be specified to make the distinction between disease morbidity levels and need for services. For example, other useful variables might be accessible indicators of social disorganization, such as homicide and suicide rate, additional family composition information, and some supplementary income variable like percentage poor on welfare. Other variables suggested could include some such as per capita hospital facilities, clinic services available, or other forms of ambulatory services, and also measures of actual use. The ratio of private physicians to population is not a sufficient indicator of provision of health services. Private medical service is provided on some money exchange basis, and so it is hardly surprising that virtually all of the variance of the physician in private practice is correlated with the health area income level.

With regard to some health indicators, additional structural variables may need to be considered. For example, there is no way of knowing from the data whether the loading on late or no pre-natal care in Factor III' is a function of the behavior of patients per se, or a lack of availability of services differentially used by particular income groups. Such information might be obtainable from normal reporting of numbers of facilities and personnel; but in order to interpret process, more subtle types of information would have to be added. For example, it is possible to visualize two health areas where facilities and health service delivery personnel seem equivalent in number, but where the organization of the delivery of services is quite different. Organization of the delivery system can involve differences in ease of making appointments, time spent waiting for examinations, and other things that may be reflected in utilization behavior. Health delivery organization might be the critical element, but, unless accounted for, differences in use might be misinterpreted as "health habits" of the clients rather than as a function of the system of delivery.

In short, the selection of variables for the original study may require augmentation, and the selection of the proxy variable probably represents a premature oversimplification. Nevertheless, Israel and Roosma's approach is not only a reasonable one but also one for which there is strong precedent. Here we have arrived at a structure that lends itself to a "needs" interpretation that is quite direct. First, there is one principle of ordering (Factor I') which corresponds to social-economic status, and this surely makes sense as a way of defining need. Since the medical indicators also occur in this variable, medical need can be served in this way. The other two factors can, net of social economic status, lead to additional orderings that imply categories of need. Factor II' suggests content for which the disorganization variables are important definers and could be viewed as other indicators of health need, particularly of services that might alter conditions and improve health. By contrast, Factor III' identifies areas of high proportions of degenerative diseases presumably associated with age. Such diseases may not be alterable in the sense that communicable diseases are, but they still may be appropriate for provision of services oriented to providing supportive palliatives. What has been added by the reanalysis presented here is an emphasis on the need for sequential studies, further consideration of the component elementary variables to be included, and a questioning of the basic assumption that a single Index of Medical Underutilization is justified.

REFERENCES

Health Services Research Group (1975) "Development of the index of medical underservice." Health Services Research 10: 168-180.

ISRAEL, M. and H. ROOSMA (1976) "Determining the critical health problem areas of New York City." Statistics and Health Review 2: 27-34.

KLEINMAN, J. C. and R. W. WILSON (1977) "Are 'medically underserved areas' medically underserved." Health Services Research 12: 147-162.

WYSONG, J. A. (1975) "The index of medical underservice: problems in meaning, measurement, and use." Health Services Research 10: 127-135.

Edgar F. Borgatta is on the faculties of the graduate programs of Sociology and of Social Psychology and Personality at the CUNY Graduate Center. He is research director of the CASE Center for Gerontological Studies and training director of an interdisciplinary program on gerontological studies.

Marie L. Borgatta is currently working on a Ph.D. Dissertation in medical sociology on social and psychological determinants of health services utilization.